Divine Analogies

Reflections at the Intersection of Faith and Modern Life

Volume 1

52 Weekly Reflections

Charles D. (Chuck) Vollmer

Published by Jobenomics Publishing, Vienna, Virginia, United States.

ISBN: 979-8-9938170-0-2

Library of Congress Control Number: Pending

Scripture quotations, unless otherwise noted, are from the Holy Bible. Public domain.

This book is part of the Divine Analogies Series, which explores parallels between spiritual principles, economic systems, and community development.

The views expressed in this book are those of the author and do not necessarily represent the views of affiliated organizations, partners, or institutions.

The information contained in this book is for educational and informational purposes only. While every effort has been made to ensure accuracy, the author and publisher assume no responsibility for errors or omissions or for damages resulting from the use of the information contained herein.

Printed in the United States of America.

First Edition.

Visit our websites:

https://DivineAnalogies.org

https://Jobenomics.org

Divine Analogies
Introduction

Reflections at the Intersection of Faith and Modern Life

Divine Analogies is a thought-provoking collection of spiritual reflections that explores timeless biblical truths through the lens of contemporary metaphors. In a world often distracted by speed, technology, and surface-level certainty, this book invites readers to pause, reflect, and reconnect with the deeper realities of faith.

Each entry in this series pairs a modern-day analogy—from data centers to fractured mirrors, from Wi-Fi to workshop benches—with a spiritual insight grounded in Scripture. These analogies serve as bridges between the visible and the invisible, helping readers see how God moves not just in ancient texts, but in the mechanics of daily life.

Rather than preach or persuade, *Divine Analogies* takes an introspective and personal approach. Each essay is written from the perspective of someone who is learning—sometimes slowly, often imperfectly—how to recognize the hand of God in unexpected places. This is not a book of theology or doctrine; it is a book of lived experience, drawn from decades of leadership, personal transformation, and quiet moments of conviction.

The analogies span a wide range of themes: faith as signal strength, sin as distortion, pride as a mountain, and Jesus as both the carpenter and the cornerstone. Some reflections are inspired by global experiences, such as standing beside a Muslim in prayer on a city street. Others are grounded in my struggles with doubt, direction, or identity.

What unites these entries is a single premise: that God is constantly communicating through nature, technology, relationships, memory, and even failure. The challenge is not His silence but our reception.

Written with humility, clarity, and deep respect for the spiritual journey of others, *Divine Analogies* is meant to spark personal reflection, group discussion, and a more grounded understanding of faith in everyday life. It is equally suited for the curious seeker, the seasoned believer, and anyone navigating the tension between the sacred and the secular.

This volume aims to be the first in an ongoing series of 52 weekly reflections—one for each week of the year—offering a rhythm of insight, reorientation, and quiet challenge for those who desire a closer walk with God.

Chuck Vollmer

God as an Atom

God created the universe, encompassing both the spiritual and material realms. In the material domain, HE likely started with an atom, the building block of the physical world, in HIS image before making humanity in HIS image.

Much like an atom, which consists of a nucleus, protons, neutrons, and electrons working in perfect harmony, God, in His fullness, embodies the Holy Trinity—Father, Son, and Holy Spirit. Each aspect of the Holy Trinity has a distinct role, yet all exist as one, inseparable and essential. The atom serves as the  fundamental building block of creation, just as God is the foundation of all existence. This parallel extends not only to the universe but also to our individual lives, illustrating how divine order is woven into the very fabric of reality.

At the heart of every atom lies the nucleus, a dense core that defines the atom's identity and provides its stability. Protons carrying a positive charge establish the atomic structure, while neutrons maintain cohesion, ensuring balance. Likewise, God the Father is the central source of divinity, the foundation upon which all things rest. He is the eternal anchor, holding the Trinity together, just as the nucleus binds the atom. Without the nucleus, the atom would disintegrate; without the Father, there would be no divine order.

Neutrons, though neutral in charge, are vital to an atom's stability. They prevent protons from repelling each other, thereby maintaining unity within the nucleus. This beautifully mirrors Jesus' role as the mediator between God and humanity. Through His sacrifice, Jesus reconciles us to the Father, bridging the gap that sin has created. His presence fosters peace, preventing division and ensuring spiritual stability. Just as neutrons hold the atom together, Christ holds our faith together, making salvation possible through His boundless grace.

Electrons, constantly in motion, surround the nucleus and enable interactions between atoms, sparking reactions that sustain life. This ceaseless energy parallels the Holy Spirit, who moves dynamically, guiding, empowering, and transforming believers. The Holy Spirit is God's active presence in the world—comforting, convicting, and connecting us to divine truth. In Jewish tradition, the Spirit is often associated with the Shekinah Glory, the manifest presence of God. Just as electrons bring vitality to matter, the Holy Spirit breathes life into our souls, leading us into deeper communion with God.

The structure of the atom reflects the divine nature of God Himself. The Father, as the nucleus, establishes identity and foundation. Jesus, as the neutron, brings harmony and reconciliation. The Holy Spirit, as the electron, fosters movement and connection. This profound analogy reveals that just as atoms are the essence of creation, God is the essence of all existence. In Him, through Him, and by Him, everything holds together—both in the universe and in our hearts.

Jesus as the First Word & Light

There is a profound mystery in the opening lines of Scripture: "In the beginning God created the heavens and the earth... And God spoke, 'Let there be light,' and there was light" (Genesis 1:1–3).

For years, I read this as the start of physical creation—until a more profound truth came into view. What if the first Word God spoke into the void was not merely sound, but a Person? What if, in speaking light into being, the Father was revealing His Son—Jesus—as the First Word and co-Creator, the divine radiance breaking into the darkness?

John's Gospel makes this connection unmistakable: "In the beginning was the Word, and the Word was with God, and the Word was God...Through Him all things were made... And the Word became flesh and made His dwelling among us" (John 1:13, 14). Jesus was not an afterthought or late arrival—He was present from the first moment, the living Word through whom all creation came into being. The Father, who is Spirit, manifested Himself through the Son, making the invisible God visible, tangible, and active in His world.

The Word came as light—not just photons or cosmic illumination, but divine clarity, the unveiling of truth and purpose. When God said, "Let there be light," He didn't only mark the beginning of time; He declared the presence of Jesus, the Light of the world (John 8:12). His light reveals what is hidden, guides the wanderer, and overcomes the darkness that sinfulness and fear bring.

This truth isn't just theological—it's deeply personal. I've known seasons of spiritual blindness, confusion, and darkness. But when Jesus entered my heart, it was as if the same voice that commanded light at the beginning now spoke directly to me: "Let there be light." And there was. His presence dispelled my shadows. His truth gave me spiritual insight and a sense of purpose.

Understanding Jesus as both the First Word and the Light changes how I see creation, history, and myself. He is not a distant religious figure—He is the origin and sustaining force of all things. The same divine power that formed galaxies also reshapes my heart. The same Light that pierced the primeval dark still shines in me today. Furthermore, Revelation 22:13 records Jesus saying, "I am the Alpha and the Omega, the First and the Last, the Beginning and the End."

Jesus was not created. He is the Word spoken before time. He is the Light that reveals, the Life that redeems, and the Presence that remains. In Him, I find both my beginning and my becoming. The voice that said "Let there be light" still speaks—illuminating everything in both the spiritual and material realms, from the first breath of creation to the final chapter of eternity.

Uncomfortable as a Bleacher Seat

There's a peculiar kind of discomfort that settles in when you've been sitting too long in the bleachers of faith. It's not physical—although the seat grows hard and uncomfortable. It's spiritual. A slow ache. A quiet hollowness. The kind that creeps in when you know you were meant for more, but you've grown used to less.

I spent years in those seats. I knew the verses, the catechisms, and church politics. I affirmed the truth, admired the players, and offered commentary from a safe distance. I was a fan of Jesus, not a follower. And fans, I've learned, can cheer without ever changing.

As a fan, I was elevated, removed from the mess. I could see the field without stepping into it. Applaud sacrifice without making any. Critique the game without risking injury. But over time, that comfort turned sour. The seat that once felt safe began to pinch. The view that once inspired began to convict. I started to notice the gap between belief and obedience—and it wasn't small.

I made it mandatory for my family to attend church on Christmas and Easter, and we would have dinner afterward. I wore the colors of faith but never surrendered. I never picked up a cross—except maybe the little ones made from palm leaves, discarded after Palm Sunday. I figured I was saved, and that was enough. An entry-level position in heaven still beat the hot seat in hell I knew I deserved.

After a decade in the bleachers, Christ called me to the field—again and again. I resisted. He never forced me. But the longer I delayed, the more I quenched His fire. That old emptiness crept back in, and hollowness frightened me more than hell ever had. So, I compromised. I didn't volunteer for varsity—I offered myself as a waterboy, maybe a second-stringer on the junior squad. I raised my hand meekly. And He accepted it, graciously.

The playing field is a lot different than the bleachers. It's not polished or predictable. It's rugged, uneven, and real. Down here, faith is not a theory—it's a testimony. You don't just know—you go. You don't just believe—you bleed. Christ didn't call me to admire Him. He called me to follow Him, not as a straggler but as part of the team. To leave comfort. Get dirty, yuck. To risk rejection. To carry burdens not my own. The  invitation was never to observe His Gospel, but to embody it.

And that's where I found Him—not in the bleachers, but in the trenches fighting evil and doing good works. He didn't want me as a fan cheering from the bleachers. He wanted me as a partner on a lifelong road trip on an eternal playing field.

Walk Worthy as My Calling, Part I

"I, therefore, the prisoner of the Lord, beseech you that ye walk worthy of the vocation wherewith ye are called." Ephesians 4:1

Every time I read Paul's words, I feel a quiet tug—not toward accomplishment, but toward surrender and compliance. "Walk worthy" is not a command but an invitation to walk in a way that reflects the One who called me into various vocations and ministries.

Jesus was a carpenter. Paul made tents. Their daily vocations served their needs. But their real lives—what endured—were shaped by ministries. That distinction has grown clearer for me over the years. My vocations—military and corporate—paid the bills. But what marked my life, shaped my soul, and tested my faith were the callings Jesus handed me.

I came into adulthood carrying wounds from a troubled childhood and, later, the weight of combat trauma. I didn't present as someone qualified for ministry—not as an ordained minister, but as an unqualified layperson. I responded, one call at a time. And somehow, despite my limits—or perhaps because of them—He kept using me.

Ministering to family and friends was the first layer. Then came more formal assignments. Over the past five decades, Jesus directed me into four lay ministries: Eschatology, Islamic Cultural Engagement, Jobenomics, and now Divine Analogies. The details belong in the following reflection, but this is where the journey began—with a willingness to shift from career to calling, from credentials to conviction.

I didn't arrive in any of these seasons polished or prepared. Yet, the call remained. Jesus didn't demand perfection, only presence. It reminded me not to measure calling by magnitude, but by obedience. What transpired was beyond anything I would have imagined—an unexpected adventure into the unknown, among people and nationalities quite unlike me, traveling to over fifty countries.

Paul's list of attributes—lowliness, meekness, patience, love, unity—did not come naturally. I had to learn how to listen longer than I felt comfortable, how to let grace lead my instincts, and how to stumble gracefully. Unlike Paul, I never proselytized or converted anyone that I remember. However, God provided me platforms where I shared my relationship with Jesus— both directly and indirectly—to millions of people.

To walk worthily, I've come to learn, is about seeking God's will and purpose for His glory, not mine. When I do this, He continues to provide me with interesting vocations and ministries—like my newest calling, Divine Analogies. This paper will be one of 52 analogies, one for each week of the year, in Volume I of seven planned volumes, God willing, as He instructed.

Walk Worthy as My Calling, Part II

"...walk worthy of the vocation wherewith ye are called." — Ephesians 4:1

Reflecting on the last five decades, I can trace the steps that took me from vocational effort into spiritual calling. Jesus didn't change my job title—He changed my purpose. The callings weren't grand entrances. They were directions received in quiet moments. In each case, I didn't feel qualified. I followed where I was led.

The first calling began in the 1980s with a growing conviction: Jesus is the Messiah. That truth didn't just stir belief—it stirred action. I studied eschatology intensely, not out of curiosity, but out of urgency. I lectured in places like Washington D.C., Dallas, Jerusalem, and Abu Dhabi, and wrote extensively. My most recent work—a detailed analysis titled "The Israel–Iran Crisis From an Eschatological Perspective" (2024–2025)—was submitted to U.S. Defense Department officials and Congress, not for recognition but because the message burned in me too strongly to ignore.

After 9/11, Jesus pointed me toward another assignment: engaging Islam and Muslims. For over a decade, I worked with U.S. Central Command, traveling more than fifty times to the Middle East and the Levant. In rooms filled with Arab royalty, generals, clerics, and Western flag officers, I conducted a dozen conferences on coalition building, including a Cultural Symposium where diplomacy and theology intersected. Privately, I engaged in hundreds of long one-on-one conversations with Muslim officials, sharing truths from the Quran about Isa bin Maryam (Jesus, son of Mary) with respect, drawing connections that planted seeds rather than stirred debate.

In 2010, another ministry emerged—this time focused on economic dignity. Jobenomics began as a quiet conviction: social mobility is fueled by economic parity. What started as a book became a global grassroots movement, helping people in underserved communities launch startup businesses and build generational change. Over 100 chapters have taken root across four continents, driven by the belief that small enterprises can spark transformation. Again, I didn't expect this. But the Lord had plans, and I kept walking worthily.

Most recently, I've been called into Divine Analogies, a ministry of contemplation and storytelling. I'm writing seven books, each offering 52 analogies—one for each week of the year. These reflections are drawn from everyday moments and anchored in eternal truths. They aren't sermons. They're sincere meditations, spoken plainly and offered generously.

Through each ministry, I've never stopped being a combat veteran with lingering PTSD, or a man shaped by a difficult childhood. But those parts of me were never disqualifying. If anything, they kept me honest. Jesus doesn't call the qualified—He qualifies the called.

Life as a Test

I've come to believe that life on Earth is not primarily about achievement, comfort, or even survival. It's about testing.

Scripture says, "God tests our hearts" (1 Thess 2:4). The very word test comes from the Latin testum—an earthen vessel used for refining precious metals. That image resonates with me. I am one of those vessels, formed from dust, shaped for a purpose, and placed in this world to be tested.

Jesus came as the Father's perfect vessel to show us how to pass these tests—not just through His teachings but by His example. My own tests reveal whether I will glorify God or serve myself. When I choose His way, I'm transformed "from one degree of glory to another" into the image of His Son (2 Cor 3:18).

Testing is not incidental in Scripture; it's central. God led Israel through the wilderness to test their hearts (Deut 8:2). Jesus Himself was led by the Spirit into the desert to be tested by Satan (Matt 4:1). And I, too, have been tested by trials, temptations, and seasons of dryness, learning if my roots are deep or shallow, like Jesus' parable of the sower (Luke 8:13).

These tests have refined me. They teach perseverance and shape me to become more like Christ (Jas 1:3). God promises not to test me beyond what I can bear (1 Cor 10:13) and equips me to "test everything" so I will not be deceived (1 Thess 5:21). "Having stood the test," I trust I will receive the crown of life (Jas 1:12).

All created beings—angels and humans—are tested to choose light or darkness. Lucifer, once radiant, failed his test, exalting himself and being cast down. Since then, Satan's goal has been to blind us from "the light of the gospel of the glory of Christ" (2 Cor 4:4).

Jesus, in His humanity, allowed Himself to be tested, even tempted by Satan to trade worship for worldly power. He did not yield. He passed every test perfectly, blazing a trail for me to follow.

I now see Earth as a divine workshop for those bound for heaven. Before I was born, God knew me (Jer 1:5), and predestined me to be conformed to the image of Christ (Rom 8:29). Although I am currently lower than the angels (Heb 2:7), if I persevere, I will one day judge them (1 Cor 6:3).

Satan offers fleeting pleasures—power, pride, possessions. God offers eternal fruit: love, peace, faithfulness, and joy (Gal 5:22-23). Many take the easy path, but the narrow road leads to life. If I endure (that is why He is called the Suffering Christ, a central theme in Christian theology) and am judged worthy, I will enter the kingdom of His beloved Son (Col 1:13). I believe this is why I am here.

Kenosis as God's Divine Plan

Kenosis refers to the doctrine of Christ's "self-emptying" in His incarnation. It is the foundational theme of God's redemptive plan. Philippians 2:7 states Jesus "emptied Himself," taking the form of a servant. He remained fully God yet lived fully human—modeling the way of obedience, dependence, and trust. To me, voluntary self-renunciation makes Jesus even more worth following—a King who chose to fight on the front lines as a common soldier. Even more mind-bending than I can perceive, His Father, with whom Jesus is One, likewise became a human and died for His creation in an ultimate act of humility.

By emptying Himself, Jesus's miracles were not displays of autonomous power. They were acts of Spirit-led obedience. He waited on the Father, prayed before acting, and did not perform wonders for personal gain. His kenosis demonstrated willing restraint, not weakness—not a lack of power, but submission to the Father's plan to redeem and adopt humanity.

Kenosis is the posture that unlocks divine partnership. It is the emptying of personal ambition, pride, and control so that God's will can flow freely. Jesus lived this way from birth to resurrection. Even in death, He did not grasp at power. He trusted the Father, and the Spirit raised Him from the dead (Rom 8:11). That moment wasn't just victory—it was vindication of the kenotic path.

This way of living wasn't just for Jesus—it was for His disciples, then and now. He said, "You will do even greater things" (Jn 14:12), but the path to that power was clear: surrender. We cannot move mountains unless it is

God's will. And if it is His will, He will enable us to do marvelous things—not through our strength, but through His Spirit.

When Jesus sent His disciples out, they carried authority but often lacked faith. Throughout the Gospels, Jesus repeatedly showed them how Spirit  power flows best through surrendered, self-empty vessels. Fortunately, the disciples eventually understood. At Pentecost, the Spirit came to indwell them as a gift to fill their openness. The disciples, emptied of fear and pride, became vessels of divine power. That same Spirit is available to me. But the condition remains: I must empty myself of self-will and focus solely on God's will.

Kenosis is not a one-time act—it is a way of life. It is the daily decision to yield, to listen, to trust. It is the path Jesus walked, and the one He invites humanity to follow. In a world obsessed with control and self-expression, kenosis calls His disciples to quiet strength, holy restraint, and access to a source of awesome power used solely to glorify God.

This is God's divine plan: that power would be perfected in weakness, that glory would come through humility, and that resurrection would follow surrender. To live in the kenotic way is to participate in that plan—not by striving, but by yielding.

Jesus as a Human

I've spent years reflecting on why Jesus chose to come to earth as a humble carpenter instead of a powerful ruler. As the only begotten Son of God, he could have arrived in glory. But he set aside his divine privileges and lived as one of us, subject to pain, disappointment, and every challenge that comes with being a commoner.

Scripture gives clear reasons for his choice: he came to do the will of God (John 6:38), save sinners (Matt 1:21), bring light to a dark world (John 12:46), share in suffering (Heb 2:14), invite others to share in God's nature (2 Pet 1:4), open the way to heaven (John 14:6), and fulfill and renew God's covenants (Jer 31:31, Luke 22:20).

God gave me free will to choose between temporary pleasures and eternal purpose. Jesus, described as the image of the invisible God (Col 1:15), came to show what it looks like to do the Father's will in real life. By enduring the same temptations and hardships I face, he modeled how faith and good works—empowered by the Holy Spirit—help me overcome evil.

One of Jesus' most important aspects of his life is that he didn't use his divine rights to dominate or demand obedience. Instead, he showed humility, earning the authority to judge humanity and declare, "No one comes to the Father except through me."

I also think it's crucial to correct a misunderstanding that I held as an early Christian, that only Christians can know God. If they did, infants, children of non-Christian parents, or those who had never heard the Gospel would be excluded. However, Jesus taught me that unless we become like little children, I can't enter the kingdom of heaven (Matt 18:3). Scripture also reminds me that those led by God's Spirit are God's children (Rom 8:14), regardless of their background.

What stands out most to me is how Jesus validated the old covenants—promises God made with Adam, Noah, Abraham, Moses, and David—while establishing a new covenant based on grace through faith in his death and resurrection. He rejected the old belief that God is just a distant master and we're merely enslaved. Instead, he revealed God as a loving Father who wants a relationship with us.

I've come to see earthly life as a test of what I truly value: spiritual qualities like love, patience, kindness, and self-control, or worldly pursuits like power, prestige, passion, possessions, and pride. Jesus was the only one to pass this test perfectly, remaining sinless. But by taking on humanity's sin at the Cross, he became the ultimate sacrifice as the ultimate sinner, allowing humankind to be reconciled with God.

Ultimately, I believe Jesus came not only to save me but to prove His obedience to His Father's will and purpose. He showed His followers how to rely on the Holy Spirit to turn toward the light of God and away from the darkness of the world. His life offers me a clear, living example of how to choose faith, follow God's will, and experience true life—now and for eternity — in a place He has already prepared for His followers.

Jesus as an Imposter

As the title implies, it was difficult for me even to suggest—let alone write—that Jesus could have been an imposter, or worse yet, a liar. Those words clash against everything I now believe. But I begin here not to provoke, but to confront the depth of my past disbelief.

As someone who has taken lives in combat, who has flown almost two hundred missions in an F-4E Phantom—a machine that carried more bombs than a B-17 in World War II—the resurrection of Christ doesn't land on me as merely a theological claim. It comes as a personal confrontation with life and death itself, a matter of no triviality to one so profoundly impacted by this topic.

Jesus's resurrection is the central tenet of Christianity. It's not symbolic or metaphorical—it's literal. If He is not risen, then our faith is in vain. For years, I lived with that tension: saying I believed yet denying its implications. I knew the stories—Jesus raising Lazarus, the boy in Nain—and His disciples raising the dead.

Deep down, I questioned whether those resurrections were real. Jesus' Bread of Life discourse was so challenging that it triggered a mass departure of disciples when He stated, "Whoever eats my flesh and drinks my blood has eternal life, and I will raise them up at the last day." (John 6:54) If so many disciples no longer believed in Him, how could I if I had lingering doubts about literally raising people from the grave. Doubt is not easy to admit. But honesty matters especially when eternity is at stake.

Jesus said, "I am the resurrection and the life." He didn't say He knew the way—He is the way. He declared that death would not have the final word, that those who believed in Him, even though they die, will live. Either that's true, or it isn't. Either He conquered death... or He didn't.

What shifted my belief wasn't just intellectual study—it was years of walking in His footsteps, figuratively in prayer and study, and literally through the landscapes of Israel and Jordan. Slowly, steadily, the weight of evidence, history, and grace broke through my skepticism. And somewhere between my trek across Israel and the stillness of my own reflection, I stopped asking whether Jesus was lying—and started trusting that He never has.

By the power of the Holy Spirit, who now resides in me, Jesus' resurrection proves that the grave is not our destination. It's a passage—a veil. And when my doubt gave way, a veil was also removed from my eyes. While I still see through a glass darkly and know in only part (1 Cor 13:12), I assert confidently that Jesus is not an imposter. He is the Truth. And after a lifetime of flying high, falling hard, and diving into Scriptures, I don't just believe He rose from the dead. I believe He'll raise me, too.

Jesus as God

After Vietnam, I returned home deeply skeptical of large institutions—government, media, and even the church. War doesn't just scar the body; it strips illusions. I didn't reject the idea of God outright, but I certainly wasn't ready to accept institutional religion's claims about Jesus. If he were God, I needed more than tradition. I needed evidence.

In 1977, stationed at Yokota Air Base in Japan, I hit a spiritual crossroads. One night, alone with my doubts, I asked God to prove He was real, not in defiance, but in genuine need. He did. What followed wasn't a flash of lightning or booming voice—but an undeniable presence.

From there, I began to investigate—not out of obligation, but with the curiosity of a soldier-turned-seeker. I read Scripture with fresh eyes and started studying how the early church defined Jesus. What struck me was how seriously they wrestled with His identity—not as theologians playing word games, but as eyewitnesses struggling to describe something extraordinary. They saw, touched, and followed someone they knew was more than a man.

My breakthrough came while exploring the historic creeds. The Apostles' Creed laid a foundation. The Nicene Creed (325 AD) boldly declared Jesus as "true God from true God." But it was the Shield of the Trinity—a 6th-century diagram tied to the Athanasian Creed—that opened my eyes to the logic behind the mystery. It

revealed a near three-dimensional relationship: Father, Son, and Holy Spirit—all God, yet distinct persons. The Son is not the Father, the Father is not the Spirit, but each is God. It didn't answer every question, but it made belief intellectually and spiritually plausible.

In 1980, I traveled to Israel—not as a pilgrim, but as a skeptic with a map in hand. I walked from Galilee to Jerusalem, stood on the Mount of Beatitudes, crossed the Jordan into Petra, and climbed Masada. Geography made Jesus real to me. He wasn't just a doctrine—He had dirt on His feet and purpose in His steps. That trip didn't convert me, but it rooted the incarnation in history.

The final turning point came when I read Philippians 2:6-7: "Though he was in the form of God, he did not count equality with God a thing to be grasped but emptied himself..." That concept, emptying himself (kenosis), pierced me. Jesus didn't surrender His divinity, but He set aside His divine privileges to become one of us. Then I read Jesus' own words: "I and the Father are one" (John 10:30). And again: "Before Abraham was, I am" (John 8:58). He wasn't hinting—He was declaring. The same "I AM" who spoke from the burning bush was standing in human flesh.

That was the kind of God I could follow. Today, I no longer ask, Is Jesus God? I ask, How can I live in light of that truth? From Yokota to Jerusalem, from skepticism to surrender—my answer is simple: Jesus is not just the Son of God. He is God.

Jesus as a Touchstone

Most Christians are familiar with Jesus as the cornerstone, the foundational stone upon which faith is built. From my perspective, Jesus as a "touchstone" is another equally powerful metaphor.

A touchstone is a stone used to test the purity of gold. When gold is rubbed against it, the streak left behind reveals whether the metal is genuine or counterfeit. In the same way, Jesus tests the authenticity of my faith. His life and teachings provide the standard against which all truth, righteousness, and spiritual integrity are measured. Just as a physical touchstone exposes impurities, Jesus gently reveals what in me still needs cleansing. He does not shame but purifies. Even the briefest contact with Him has the power to refine.

The story of the woman who touched Jesus' garment offers a vivid image of this kind of encounter. I picture her: frail, exhausted by years of affliction, threading her way through the crowd with quiet desperation. She wasn't reaching for cloth—she was reaching for wholeness.

One touch of His garment heals. Not just the body, but emotions, mind, and soul. I know this firsthand. The weight I've carried—old regrets, hidden fears—begins to lift in His presence.

One touch redeems. Where I once wandered without clarity or conviction, I now walk with purpose. My steps have more meaning, aligned with a path lit by His truth.

One touch reconciles and atones. The separation between God and me, shaped by my flaws and failings, is erased daily. Jesus' death and resurrection built a bridge where there had only been a chasm.

One touch justifies. What once marked me as guilty is now covered by grace. The heavenly host no longer judges me as an enemy of God now that the Holy Father accepts me as His child.

One touch transforms. The Spirit of Christ does not leave me unchanged. Over time, my patterns shifted. My thoughts softened. My desires realigned. I grow—not perfectly, but persistently—into the type of disciple that God created me to be in Christ Jesus.

In this world, many voices claim to define truth, but only One can purify it. Jesus, as a touchstone, does not simply reveal what I am; He shows me what I can become. He tests, yes—but always with love, always with the invitation to be more. And in the quiet moments of contact, when my life brushes up against His, I'm reminded that transformation doesn't come from striving but from surrendering to the One whose touch is holy.

Jesus as a Frustrated Shepherd

Faith is about hoping for things unseen and trusting in promises yet to be fulfilled. Feelings, on the other hand, are rooted in the present—fluid, unpredictable, and easily manipulated. Over the years, I've come to recognize how emotions can become speed bumps on Jesus' righteous path, pulling me away from the certainty of faith. But I've also learned that Jesus—my Shepherd, Mentor, and Master—walked this same road. He dealt with frustration, sorrow, and even moments of deep anguish, yet remained sinless, empowered by the Holy Spirit, showing me the way forward.

Jesus, in His fully human nature, felt deeply. The hypocrisy of religious leaders angered Him. The stubbornness of the people He longed to save saddened Him. He grew frustrated when His disciples failed to grasp the truth. He wept, groaned in spirit, and cried out in anguish. Yet, in all of this, He never sinned. His frustration was righteous, His sorrow pure, and even His doubt was met with surrender to the Father's will.

One of the clearest examples of Jesus' frustration came when He cleansed the temple—overturning tables and driving out merchants who had turned God's house into a marketplace. This wasn't blind rage—it was righteous anger, a defense of holiness. It was the Shepherd protecting His flock from corruption. If Jesus, the Perfect One, felt this kind of frustration, I need not be ashamed of mine. The question is how I handle whether I let it become a tool of the enemy or surrender it to the refining work of the Spirit.

Jesus didn't just face frustration in the temple. His life was marked by moments of exasperation and sorrow. He healed on the Sabbath despite the Pharisees' rigid legalism, rebuked their hypocrisy, and became indignant when His disciples prevented children from coming to Him. He grieved over Jerusalem's rejection, corrected Peter, and sighed in disappointment when His disciples failed to understand His teaching. But the most heart-wrenching moments of His humanity came in Gethsemane. On the cross, when He cried out in anguish. He felt the weight of separation from His Father. Each moment reveals Jesus, the frustrated Shepherd, navigating human emotion without ever succumbing to sin.

Perhaps the most profound lesson Jesus teaches is that faith must triumph over feelings. As a human, He willingly laid down His divine power (kenosis) and experienced emotion firsthand to shepherd by example.

After four decades of walking with Him, I've learned that the closer I draw to the narrow gate, the more the enemy tries to twist my emotions—to turn frustration into anger, sorrow into despair, and doubt into rebellion. But Jesus shows a better way.

And so, I stumble forward. Even when emotions cloud my vision, faith can clear the path—if I fix my eyes on the Shepherd who turns my feelings into faith.

Jesus as a Pacifist

The commandment "You shall not kill" (Exodus 20:13; Deuteronomy 5:17) is etched in stone as a moral boundary. But its meaning becomes far more complicated when you've been trained to take life to protect others. I've spent a career confronting evil with force. I know what happens when injustice goes unchecked—and what it costs to resist it.

When Jesus says, *"You have heard it said... 'You shall not murder,' but I say to you that anyone who is angry with his brother is liable to judgment"* (Matthew 5:21,22), I take notice. He's not softening the commandment—He's going deeper. He teaches that murder begins in the heart, long before the weapon is drawn.

That's a hard teaching for a combat veteran like me. If Jesus so strongly condemned internal hostility, why didn't He speak out against the external atrocities of His time? He healed the sick and raised the dead, but never blamed the state-sanctioned slaughter of His people.

He passed the rotting, mutilated bodies on crosses that lined Roman roads, but did not address their suffering. He could have challenged the Roman machine, but didn't. Instead, He preached a message of love and reconciliation with God that the Romans tried to crush under their oppressive heel. This silence has long puzzled theologians, especially given the brutality of Roman rule in Judea.

I flew 175 combat missions as the aircraft commander of a fighter-bomber that delivered more ordnance per sortie than a World War II B-17. I inflicted death and destruction—on a scale I can never entirely forget. Thousands of enemy combatants and an unknown number of innocent civilians were likely killed or wounded by the missions I led. I carried out my orders with precision and discipline, believing I was serving justice. And maybe I was.

While I mourn the lives lost in combat—both friends and foes—I do not carry guilt. I conducted myself as honorably as one can in the fog of war. But as a long-time follower of Christ, I still wrestle with how to reconcile the pacifism of the Lamb with the righteous fury of the Lion.

Some say Jesus remained silent because His mission was spiritual, not political. He didn't come to overthrow Rome, but to conquer sin. Maybe that's true. Perhaps He wasn't ignoring evil—maybe He was absorbing it. And in rising again, He redefined power, justice, and victory.

Still, I long for the Lion. Like John the Baptist—who asked, "Are You the One, or should we look for another?" (Matthew 11:3)—I struggle with Jesus' reticence to directly confront Roman cruelty. But Jesus didn't rebuke John for asking, and I trust He won't rebuke me either. But I also pray for the courage to live faithfully in the waiting—for the day the Lion returns, not just to redeem, but to restore, and to make all things right.

Jesus as Lord of the Sabbath

For years, I've wrestled with how to observe the Sabbath properly. I've tried to set Sundays aside as sacred—carving out time for worship, rest, and family—but too often, the day slipped by, overtaken by routine. It wasn't rebellion, just life pressing in. Recently, in prayer, I sensed a gentle correction—not a rebuke, but a redirection. The Spirit of the Lord spoke clearly to my heart, "Jesus is the Lord of the Sabbath, not the other way around." This simple truth meant that the Sabbath is less about securing one day for religious reflection and more about learning to walk with the Lord of the Sabbath in my everyday life.

Jesus said, "The Sabbath was made for man, not man for the Sabbath." (Mark 2:27-28). When Jesus walked the earth, He didn't observe the Sabbath the way the Pharisees expected. He healed, taught, defended the hungry, and showed mercy, all of which was anything but restful, demonstrating that the heart of the Sabbath is not inactivity but alignment with God's will.

Most people associate Sabbath with not working on Sunday because God "rested" on the seventh day. But God wasn't tired—He stopped because His work was complete. His rest was about satisfaction, not recovery. The Hebrew word Shabbat means "to cease" doing the ordinary to reflect on the extraordinary—God's goodness, power, and provision.

In the Old Testament, the Sabbath served as a reminder to Israel of their Creator and their Liberator. In the New Testament, Jesus embodies both. He doesn't abolish the Sabbath—He fulfills it. And in doing so, He shows me that rest is ultimately found in Him.

Over time, I've come to realize that I need "sabbaticals" not just once a week but woven throughout my days. A few moments of stillness in the morning. A pause in the middle of a chaotic afternoon. A walk, a prayer, a deep breath. These are small sabbaticals—interruptions that reorient me from the noise of the world back to the voice of the Lord. This perspective doesn't diminish the Sabbath—it expands it.

Now, I treat Sundays as a gift, not a weight. A chance to gather with those I love—at church, at home, out in nature. It's also an opportunity to find refreshment in doing simple things alongside my Lord. Even yard work becomes sacred when I'm aware He's with me. The joy isn't in checking a religious box—it's in walking with the One who offers rest that no schedule can hold.

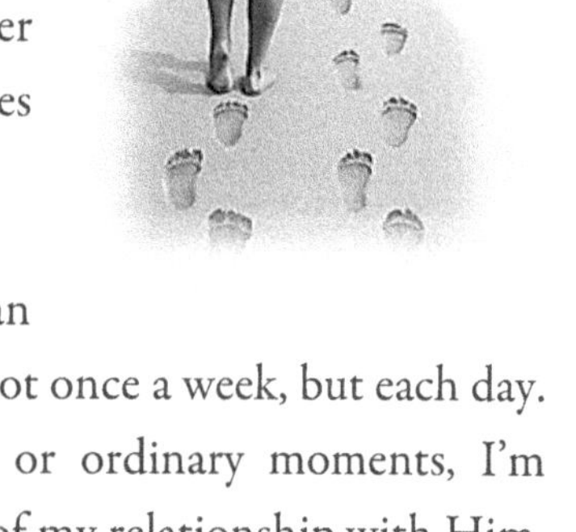

That image of footsteps beside the still water reminds me that it's not my stride that secures Sabbath—it's He who walks with me.

Each pause, each breath of reflection, is an invitation to honor the Lord of the Sabbath not once a week, but each day. Whether through worship, service, silence, or ordinary moments, I'm learning to receive rest as a fundamental part of my relationship with Him. In the silence of rest, I can see and hear Him more clearly.

Seeking as a Lifelong Pursuit

If there's one word that has steadily reshaped my understanding of faith, it's "seek." The King James Bible uses "seek" over 300 times and "seeking" close to 30—tucked into verses about wisdom, justice, peace, and, above all, the presence of God.

Seeking isn't something I once did to "find" God. It's how I return to Jesus—day after day. Early in my walk with Christ, I assumed that faith would eventually produce clarity—a kind of spiritual autopilot where maturity would make hard questions fade. But that's not how it works. Even after years of following Him, I still wake up asking, What matters most today? Where am I drifting? What part of me resists His correction?

What comforts me is knowing God doesn't grow tired of these questions. Jesus didn't just permit persistence—He encouraged it. I think of it as holy persistence, even holy pestering. He told parables about the friend who knocks at midnight and the widow who keeps returning to the judge. They weren't about annoyance, but perseverance—not out of entitlement, but trust. Trust that God welcomes our persistence, even when it's messy.

I've experienced that firsthand. When I come to God repeatedly—asking for clarity, wisdom, or just peace—He responds. Not always with the answers I expect, and rarely on my timetable. Sometimes, it's a verse I hadn't planned to read. Other times, it's a conversation or a coincidence I can't ignore. And then there are those quiet, steady moments when I sense His presence and know I've been heard.

I've learned to see seeking not as a spiritual task to complete but as a posture to maintain. It doesn't require eloquence or certainty—just honesty and a willingness to ask again. Seeking keeps me humble. It reminds me I don't have it all figured out, and that's okay. What matters is that I keep showing up.

The Holy Spirit sharpens my pursuit. He makes me more aware of subtle nudges—moments that call for stillness, reflection, or restraint. I find myself lingering a bit longer in Scripture or listening more closely when something stirs me. Seeking, in this sense, has become less dramatic and more integrated. It's in the pause before reacting, in the second look at something I thought I understood, in the willingness to be corrected.

Seeking may not feel like progress, but it's where transformation happens. It's how I'm realigned and stay in step with the One who knows the path even when I don't. And in that daily, sometimes desperate, always welcomed pursuit—I remember who He is, and who He is shaping me to be: the man He intended.

Faith as a Contract

Faith is a contract, one that God extends to humanity. While no force in heaven or earth can separate us from the love of Christ, Scripture warns that faith itself is something we can reject, abandon, and ultimately render null and void. The mercy of God is abundant, and He calls His children back time and again, but if one continually rejects Him, turns away, and blasphemes the Holy Spirit, there comes a point where faith is broken beyond return.

The Bible gives us stark warnings about this reality. 2 Peter 2:20-22 presents one of the most vivid analogies regarding those who leave the faith: "If they have escaped the corruption of the world by knowing our Lord and Savior Jesus Christ and are again entangled in it and are overcome, they are worse off at the end than they were at the beginning."

This passage is unflinching in its finality—those who return to their old ways after knowing Christ are compared to a dog returning to its vomit and a washed pig returning to the mud. The image is disturbing, but its lesson is clear: forsaking faith in Jesus and returning to the ways of the world is not just a mistake—it is a tragic regression, a rejection of the salvation freely given.

This warning is not spoken lightly. Throughout scripture, believers are urged to hold fast to faith, to endure, and to resist the lure of wealth, power, and pleasures that can lead them astray.

"For those who were once enlightened...and were made partakers of the Holy Spirit...and then fall away, it is impossible to renew them again unto repentance; seeing they crucify to themselves the Son of God afresh and put him to an open shame." Hebrews 6:4-6 (ASV) This passage warns me and others that those who have truly known Christ and then turn away could eventually forfeit their opportunity for repentance. This is not because God's mercy is limited but because their hearts have become hardened, their rejection too deep to be undone.

The temptations of the world are powerful, and earthly rewards of power, prestige, passion, and wealth are seductive. But I also know that I walk on enemy ground, and straying too far off the path of Jesus puts my soul in grave danger. Alone, I do not have the strength to remain faithful. It is only through the Holy Spirit that I can endure, resist the pull of the world, and hold fast to the covenant of faith given to me by my Savior.

Faith is more than belief—it is commitment, perseverance, and trust. It is something that can be broken, not by Christ, but by those who walk away. And though the warnings are grave, though scripture tells of those who have abandoned the faith and been lost, I pray that I will never be among them. May I never turn back to what God has rescued me from, never return to what leads to destruction. By His strength alone, I hold on, and I pray that I always will.

Faith & Trust as in Troubled Times

I've come to believe that faith and trust aren't just spiritual ideals—they're survival tools. Not the kind you pull out when things are going well, but the kind you cling to when the ground gives way beneath you. In troubled times, faith isn't ornamental. It's structural.

Psalm 46 says, "God is our refuge and strength, an ever-present help in trouble." That phrase—ever-present—has stuck with me. It doesn't say God is occasionally available or conditionally attentive. It says He's there. Always. Even when the fig tree doesn't bud, as Habakkuk puts it. Even when the outcomes we hoped for don't materialize. That's where trust begins—not in the presence of fruit, but in the confidence that the root system runs deep.

I've had seasons where everything visible seemed to contradict what I believed. Plans unraveled. People disappointed. The storm, like in Mark 4, was real. And loud. And Jesus' question to the disciples—"Why are you so afraid? Do you still have no faith?"—felt less like a rebuke and more like a mirror. I wasn't afraid because I lacked belief in God's existence. I was fearful because I doubted His proximity. I mistook silence for absence.

But faith, as Hebrews 11:1 reminds us, is the substance of things hoped for, the evidence of things not seen. It's not blind optimism. It's spiritual infrared—seeing what natural eyes can't. Trust, then, is choosing to stay tethered to that unseen anchor. Not because the storm isn't real, but because the anchor is more real.

I've learned that trust is a thermostat, not a thermometer. Isaiah 26 says, "You will keep in perfect peace those whose minds are steadfast, because they trust in you." That peace doesn't come from the absence of trouble. It comes from a decision to adjust my internal spiritual thermostat to reduce the heat of external chaos. It's not passive. It's deliberate.

When I find myself in turbulent waters, I often picture myself stranded in a small boat in a rough sea, anchored just below the surface. This boat is battered, but it doesn't drift. The anchor isn't visible, but it holds. That's what faith feels like in troubled times. Not triumphant. Not flashy. Just steady. Waiting for my Lord and Savior to come to my aid.

I don't write this as someone who's mastered trust. I write it as someone who's learning, slowly, that faith isn't about controlling outcomes. It's about surrendering to a trustworthy God. Not because I always feel it, but because I've seen enough to know He holds when everything else breaks loose.

Troubled times don't make faith irrelevant. They make it essential. And trust isn't a feeling—it's a choice to stay tethered. Even when the fig tree doesn't bud. Even when the storm doesn't stop. Even when the silence feels heavy. Anchored in Christ, I have refuge from my distress.

Fearfully as in Wonderfully Made

They say a hammer sees everything as a nail. It's a simple truth—when a tool is designed for a specific purpose, that purpose tends to shape how it perceives the world.

As a fighter pilot with 4,000 hours in the cockpit, I was trained to see through the gunsight piper—the projected point of impact crosshairs. Every movement, every flicker on the radar, every shift in the periphery was analyzed as a potential threat or target. That focus wasn't just encouraged—it was ingrained into my mindset.

But there's a danger in letting that mindset carry over into life outside the cockpit. Before I knew Jesus, I saw people the same way I saw airspace: as a field of motion, full of variables to assess and obstacles to navigate. I didn't realize it at the time, but I was living with a narrowed lens—what Paul described in 1 Corinthians 13:12 as seeing "through a glass, darkly." I wasn't seeing people for who they truly were. I was seeing shadows—outlines, not essence.

As I read Psalm 139:13-18, "You knit me together in my mother's womb. I praise you because I am fearfully and wonderfully made," this truth struck me deeply, not just about me, but about everyone. Each person I encounter—whether they lift me or wear me down—is the work of divine craftsmanship. God didn't just manufacture us; HE formed us. With intention. With tenderness. With awe.

"Fearfully" doesn't mean with terror—it means with reverence. It's the kind of awe I felt watching the sun rise over a distant horizon from 30,000 feet, where the earth seems still and silent, and the heavens unfold in grandeur. If that same awe went into forming each soul on this earth, then who am I to reduce someone to an annoyance, an opponent, or even a target?

And "wonderfully?" That means beauty. Worth. A reflection of God's creativity and care. Not flawless—we all fall short—but fearfully, wonderfully, deliberately made. God knew my failures before I ever took flight, yet He still calls me His own as long as I am with Jesus.

That truth reorients my vision. It challenges how I respond to the man who cuts me off in traffic, the clerk who seems indifferent, the colleague who pushes my buttons. They're not just random variables in my day. They are sons and daughters of the Almighty, crafted with purpose, for a divine purpose that I must respect regardless of what I may perceive or witness.

Though I misjudge, falter, and fail, God's truth never wavers. Each person I cross paths with is crafted in His image, fearfully and wonderfully made. When I embrace that reality and let it reshape how I view others, it shifts my sight-picture from mere images to their essence.

Holy Spirit as a Royal Banker

I have come to see the Holy Spirit as a royal banker—a living treasury within me, managed by Jesus and approved by the Father.

The Spirit of the Father and Jesus is no ordinary banker. He is also my counselor, caregiver, conscience, and transformer. He is not distant or theoretical; He is close, active, and deeply personal,  shaping me into a disciple who carries the aroma of Christ (2 Cor 2:15) and bears fruit that brings pleasure to my Father.

The gifts of the Spirit feel like divine deposits of heavenly resources I could never earn but have been entrusted to me through grace. Paul lists them in his letters to the Corinthians as wisdom, knowledge, faith, healing, miraculous powers, prophecy, discernment, tongues, and the gift of interpretation. His letter to the Romans adds serving, teaching, encouragement, generosity, leadership, and mercy. To the Ephesians, he listed apostles, prophets, evangelists, pastors, and teachers. These are all spiritual assets, transferred from heaven into my life account.

But deposits are only half the picture. The fruit of the Spirit—love, joy, peace, patience, kindness, goodness, faithfulness, gentleness, and self-control (Gal 5:22, 23)—are like withdrawals. They are tangible evidence that the Holy Spirit is actively at work within me. They are the visible "spending" of

God's resources in my relationships, my words, and my actions. If the gifts are the capital entrusted to me, the fruit is God's return on investment—the proof that His life is flowing through mine.

Like any account, this one requires ongoing connection with the Banker. I can't withdraw what I have ignored to receive. Jesus used the image of a vine and branches in "Abide in me... apart from me you can do nothing." (John 15:4,5) If I cut myself off from the Spirit's presence, the account may remain open, but it will lie dormant. When I yield to His leading, the flow between deposit and withdrawal is unbroken, and His life moves through mine freely, as it did through Jesus in His earthly ministry.

Seeing the Holy Spirit as a royal banker changes the way I view my days. I realize I am not operating on my own resources. My inner man has been entrusted with the wealth of heaven. My role is stewardship—to invest these gifts in service, to let them bear fruit in everyday encounters, and to let His wisdom shape each decision.

Increasingly, I find myself seeking His counsel before acting. Every wise choice, word of encouragement, or act of kindness is a transaction drawn from His limitless account. And in the end, it is not my balance sheet that matters, but the increase in His kingdom and the joy of hearing, "Well done, good and faithful servant" (Matt 25:23).

Sacrifice as an Atonement

I've wrestled for years with a troubling question: Why did God allow animal and child sacrifice to exist in His creation? If He is truly omnipotent—and I believe He is—why doesn't He prevent such evil? The answer, I've come to think, begins not on Earth but in heaven, with the casting out of Lucifer. When Satan fell, Earth became a proving ground—not just for angels, but for humanity. A place of testing. A place where each soul must choose between the light of God and the darkness of rebellion. And at the end of this age of testing, God promises a new heaven and a new Earth for those who choose Him.

From my limited, human perspective—yes, I still see through a glass darkly—this testing has always involved suffering. And sacrifice. The word *sacrifice* appears more than 300 times in Scripture. It's not incidental; it's central. And the most solemn form of sacrifice has always been the shedding of blood unto death.

From Mesopotamia and India to the Aztecs and ancient Israel, sacrifice was a central component of worship. Animal sacrifice placed guilt onto a substitute—the innocent for the guilty. Blood symbolized life, and returning it to God was a way of seeking restoration. Only the unblemished could be offered. But in many cultures, the ultimate offering was human life. Abraham's near-sacrifice of Isaac remains one of the most unsettling stories in Scripture. How could the God of love ask for such a thing?

I brought that question repeatedly before God—and the answer I sensed was one word: atonement. Atonement appears over a hundred times in the Bible. It's not just theological—it's the heartbeat of the Gospel. Jesus, the unblemished Lamb, became the ultimate substitute. Just as Abraham offered Isaac, God offered His Son. Unlike Abraham, God the Father completed the offering. Jesus' sacrifice settled my sin debt, reconciled my wrongdoings with God, and changed me from an enemy to a child of God.

With that in mind, I've come to see this age of suffering and sacrifice as temporary. God has ushered in new eras before—after Eden, after the flood, after Christ. I believe another is coming: perhaps a brief Millennial reign, followed by a new heaven and Earth.

Yes, sacrifice is painful. Atonement is costly. But they are not the end. They are means. They point to something more profound: preparation, purification, and a sense of purpose. God is preparing a place for those who seek His light—and Scripture hints that His chosen will be placed above angels, entrusted with responsibilities beyond our imagination. Jesus told His disciples they would judge the twelve tribes of Israel. That promise echoes forward.

In that, I find hope. Sacrifice is not senseless. Atonement is not cruel. They are the crucible through which God tests and draws us into His eternal purpose and everlasting life.

God as a Storehouse

A storehouse is not merely a place of storage—it is a place of preparation, abundance, and strategic allocation. In agricultural terms, it holds grain for future sustenance. In spiritual terms, God is our eternal storehouse—overflowing with all that is good, pure, and life-giving. He is not a distant supplier, but an intentional provider who knows

exactly what I need and dispenses it at His perfect timing.

I once viewed God like a genie—conjured in crisis, expected to fix problems on demand. That view almost blasphemed the vastness of His nature. Now, I see Him as the central storehouse of all power, all knowledge, and all goodness. He is not only the distributor of what is needed—He is the Creator of every resource, every truth, every spiritual gift. It's no wonder He is known as the Almighty and Majestic Glory.

Scripture affirms this image. "The Lord will open to you His good treasure, the heavens..." (Deuteronomy 28:12). He invites me to seek His will (Romans 12:2), not ours; to surrender our desires in exchange for a share in His abundance. Our access to the storehouse isn't transactional—it's relational. The more I lean into obedience, the more He entrusts me with His riches.

Jesus reminds me in Matthew 7:7 to ask, seek, and knock. These aren't passive suggestions—they're protocols for accessing heaven's inventory. And unlike worldly systems ruled by principalities, God's storehouse is filled not with pride, passion, or prestige, but with the fruits of the Spirit: love, joy, peace, patience, kindness, goodness, faithfulness, gentleness, and self-control (Galatians 5:22-23). These aren't temporary highs—they are eternal provisions that strengthen character and deepen intimacy with Him.

Take love, for example. I'm commanded to love God wholeheartedly and others more than myself (Matthew 22:37-39). I can't manufacture that kind of love—it doesn't originate in me. So, I must draw from God's storehouse. He is love (1 John 4:8). Through Christ, I receive it. By the Spirit, I distribute it. And what I give—even if imperfect—is received with grace and returned to me, purified and replenished.

It reminds me of my grandkids asking for money to buy me a gift. I delight in their request—not because I need anything—but because I love their desire to give. I provide the means, they offer the gift, and the cycle is rich with affection. Likewise, God equips me to honor Him with what already belongs to Him. I'm not earning His favor—I'm stewarding His abundance.

God's storehouse is not limited by time, scarcity, or economy. It is an inexhaustible vault of mercy, power, and grace. He invites me—and you—to come daily, not as beggars, but as sons and daughters. To receive what I cannot earn, and to give back what I did not originate.

Holy Spirit as the Shekinah Glory

Shekinah comes from a Hebrew root meaning "to dwell" or "to abide." It represents God's manifest presence, often seen in Scripture as a radiant cloud or a consuming fire. This wasn't just symbolic light; it was God drawing near in holiness and glory.

Throughout the Old Testament, the Shekinah appeared as a pillar of cloud by day and fire by night, leading the Israelites through the wilderness (Exodus 13:21–22). It filled the Tabernacle so much that even Moses couldn't enter (Exodus 40:34–35). Later, it filled Solomon's Temple so powerfully that the priests couldn't even stand to minister (1 Kings 8:10–11). These divine manifestations were not mere stories—they were declarations of God's heart to be with His people.

However, all of those appearances ultimately led to something more profound: the presence of God not just with His people, but within them.

There was a time when I thought of God's presence as distant—restricted to special places or dramatic encounters. But slowly, I've seen what Scripture reveals so clearly: the Shekinah Glory wasn't meant to visit me—it was meant to dwell in me. Through the Holy Spirit, God's presence has taken up residence in my heart—not because I am worthy, but because Christ made the way.

Still, I don't say this from a place of spiritual arrival. I feel more like Paul in Philippians 3:13-14, who admitted he had not yet attained but was pressing forward toward God's high calling in Christ Jesus. I am still being shaped, surrendering, and learning what it means to deny my will and walk in the will of the Father. And far too often, I fall short.

But the Holy Spirit—this Shekinah Glory within me—does not abandon me. He convicts me, counsels me, and comforts me. He redirects my steps when I veer off course. He transforms me, however slowly, into someone I could never become on my own.

The veil was torn through Christ, and God's presence moved from stone temples into living hearts. Though I remain a work in progress, still very much under construction, I carry this sacred truth: the Shekinah Glory has made its home in me. Not because I've earned it, but because God desires to dwell in the hearts of those who seek Him.

So, I press on—not claiming arrival but surrendering daily. I long for His light to grow brighter in me and for my life, though flawed, to reflect His glory in a world longing for the touch of the divine.

Sin as Embedded DNA

I've come to a quiet, unshakable realization: sin is embedded in my spiritual DNA as a result of the fallen nature of humankind. I admit to this malady not in a dramatic or scandalous sense, but as a steady undercurrent of who I am. Sin isn't just something I fall into occasionally; it feels woven in me, like the language my heart speaks most fluently.

This isn't a confession of some hidden shame. There's no wave of guilt or dramatic climax—just an honest awareness that my instincts are bent inward. Even when I try to do good, I find subtle threads of self-interest running through my intentions. Oddly, acknowledging this doesn't leave me in despair so much as relief since this confession pleases my Lord and Savior.

Recognizing sin is the starting point for redirection and change. I often tell my children that the difference between a good man and a bad one isn't the absence of sin, but the willingness to see it. The good man recognizes his sinful nature and fights against it; the evil man ignores it and is quietly consumed by it. I want to be the kind of person who sees my sin clearly and refuses to let it take root. Jesus' words in Scripture affirm this stark reality: "If we say we have no sin, we deceive ourselves, and the truth is not in us" (1 John 1:8).

When I read the Bible, I'm struck by how often sin appears—over four hundred mentions, depending on the translation. Jesus addressed it almost forty times in the four Gospels alone. Yet, He never spoke of it with cold detachment or harsh condemnation. His words feel personal, even tender, as if He sees the depth of our brokenness and longs to lead us out of it.

When Jesus told the woman caught in adultery, "Go, and do not sin again" (John 8), it wasn't condemnation but liberation. When He warned that "what comes out of a man" is what defiles him (Mark 7), it felt like He was shining a light directly on my thoughts and motives, revealing how natural sin is for me.

I remember my first time in Abu Dhabi, when my sponsor responded to the Muslim call to prayer by prostrating himself on the busy downtown sidewalk. I stood awkwardly by, embarrassed for him as life bustled around us. When he finished, I told him politely how uncomfortable it made me. He responded just as politely, saying he, too, felt embarrassed—*for me*. He explained that as a sinful man, the Quran commands Muslims to pray five times a day to reorient themselves to the right path. As a committed Christian, I was deeply moved by how profoundly his words resonated with me. I saw how easily my heart drifts and how desperately I need regular reorientation because I'm prone to wandering off the path expected by my Savior.

Jesus didn't come to expose sin. He came to heal it. That's why accepting sin as part of my DNA doesn't feel like defeat. It feels like the first honest step toward recalibration. Toward grace. Toward home.

Sin as a Fire Extinguisher

The Holy Spirit arrived at Pentecost not as a gentle breeze, but as a rushing wind and tongues of fire—an unmistakable sign that heaven collided with earth. That same fire, once ignited in the hearts of Jesus' disciples, now burns in me. The Holy Spirit is my counselor, my caregiver, and my source of power. But this divine flame is not immune to threat. When repeated and unrepentant, Sin acts like a fire extinguisher, dousing the Spirit's flame and severing my connection to God.

Jesus came to resolve my sin issues—not to erase them, but to redeem them. He transformed me from an enemy of God to a child of God. That transformation came with a gift: the indwelling Holy Spirit. This Spirit is my lifeline, my daily link to heaven. But sin interrupts that link. It breaks communion, threatens abundance, and endangers the place in heaven Jesus promised me. Satan's strategy is surgical. His tools—quenching, grieving, and blaspheming the Spirit—are precision strikes, designed to neutralize the fire within me.

Quenching the Spirit is subtle but deadly. It happens when I say no, deny, or delay acting on the Spirit's counsel. Paul warned, "Do not quench the Spirit" (1 Thess 5:19). He urged believers to hold fast to what is good and abstain from all forms of evil. When I rebel, even passively, I impede the Spirit's power and drift toward worldly pleasures and pride, away from my Lord.

Grieving the Spirit cuts deeper. It's not just resistance. It is sorrow inflicted on the One who sealed me for redemption. Paul again exhorts, "Do not grieve the Holy Spirit of God" (Eph 4:30). When I allow pride, bitterness, anger, or unwholesome thoughts to take root, I disrespect the Spirit. His power withdraws—not in abandonment, but in sorrow—waiting for me to turn back from the darkness and toward His flame and lighted path of Jesus.

Blaspheming the Spirit is the most severe. Jesus Himself declared "blasphemy" the unpardonable sin (Matt 12:31). He said He would forgive those who curse Him, but not those who malign the Holy Spirit—neither in this age nor the age to come. Blasphemy completely severs the lifeline. It's spiritual suicide. It's the final extinguishing of the flame.

Though sin runs through my DNA—woven into the human story since Adam's fall—the Spirit within me is no fragile flicker. It was never meant to sputter like a candle in the wind. It was meant to blaze like a bonfire of holy presence. Roaring, relentless, and not easily quenched. Flickering flames are easily doused, but a bonfire defeats even the mightiest torrents.

The good news is this: the Holy Spirit is more than my counselor and caregiver. He has become my conscience. His whisper now shouts like a megaphone in my sensitized soul. I hear Him loud and clear to resist the enemy's fire extinguishers. By choosing to live by the Spirit's fire, I choose life. Life with God is not just better—it's the only life worth living.

Faith as a WI-FI

If I've learned anything, staying connected to the Holy Spirit through Jesus is vital. I often think of it as a Wi-Fi connection that gives us spiritual access to everything we need. And just like when I am disconnected from Wi-Fi, life without that connection feels off. I am out of sync, fumbling for direction, unable to access the peace, clarity, and strength that only God can provide.

The beauty and challenge of this connection is that it's not forced. That's the way of Jesus: He invites but never compels. He gives us the freedom to stay yoked to Him or to walk away. I've come to understand, through both Scripture and experience, that every time I choose to disconnect, I risk losing my way. It's not because God closes the door but because my heart can grow cold, and the world's pull becomes harder to resist.

The Bible offers sobering lessons. 2 Peter 2:20–22 warns of the dangers of falling away after knowing Christ, using striking images: a dog returning to its vomit, a pig returning to the mud. It's harsh, but it resonates. Losing that connection feels like regression, like losing the good that God has built within us. I also think of Judas Iscariot, who betrayed Jesus, and the rich young ruler, who turned away because he couldn't let go of his grip on earthly treasures. These stories remind me how easily fear, distractions, or desires can distract us from connection with God.

Yet, even in the warnings, the Bible offers abundant hope. Peter denied Jesus three times, found forgiveness, and became a pillar of the early Church. Jonah ran from God's call but was given a second chance to fulfill his mission. Their stories—and many others—assure me that no matter how far I may stray, God's grace is always ready to meet me if I turn back.

Still, I take the warning about the risk of permanently severing that connection seriously. Jesus speaks of the unforgivable sin—blasphemy against the Holy Spirit. Repeatedly rejecting the Holy Spirit's leading and choosing our way over and over again will lead me, God forbid, to a place where I no longer hear His voice. It's not that God ever stops calling—it's that my heart could become too hardened to respond.

What I've realized is that faith isn't automatic. It's something I have to nurture, protect, and choose every day. Staying connected requires intentionality, which I achieve through prayer, immersing myself in Scripture, and walking alongside others who encourage and strengthen my faith. It's not always easy. There have been seasons when doubt, distraction, or hardship made me feel distant. But I've learned that reconnection is always possible. Like a Wi-Fi signal always broadcasting, God's Spirit is always available, waiting for me to reach out and reconnect.

If there's one thing I hold onto, it's that staying connected to the Holy Spirit isn't just important—it's life itself.

Earth as a Divine Workshop

I've come to view Earth not just as a stage for human drama or a resource for survival but as a divine workshop—crafted by God with intentionality, recreated with mercy, and destined for glory.

From the beginning, the purpose of Earth has been spiritual formation: a place where souls are shaped, tested, and prepared for eternity.

Genesis opens with a masterpiece. God created the heavens and the Earth and called it "very good." But it wasn't just beautiful—it was functional, ordered, and fertile, designed to host humanity made in His image. Earth was the workshop where we would learn to walk with God, steward creation, and choose trust over rebellion. But when Adam and Eve fell, sin corrupted the divine workshop. The tools were still there, but the work became toilsome. Yet, God did not abandon His design—He refined it.

By the time of Noah, wickedness had so saturated the human heart that God "regretted that he had made man on the earth" (Gen 6:6). But instead of eradicating the workshop, He reworked it. The Flood was not the end—it was a reset. God preserved a remnant in the ark, not just of people, but of purpose. The earth was cleansed, restructured, and re-consecrated for continued spiritual labor. The post-Flood covenant with Noah was clear: God would remain committed to humanity's formation, even though the human heart was still inclined toward evil (Gen 8:21).

Throughout history, Earth has remained the setting for God's patient craftsmanship. His covenants, prophets, miracles, and ultimately His Son have all been part of the refining process. Jesus came not to abandon the workshop but to inhabit it—working as a carpenter in His early years and as the Master Builder of eternal souls in His ministry. His death and resurrection completely retooled the process. Through Him, we are not only refined but redeemed.

Yet Scripture is clear: this current version of Earth is not the final form. The workshop itself groans under the weight of sin and decay (Rom 8:22). One day, God will create a New Heaven and a New Earth—not as a replacement, but as a perfected form, the culmination of His plan. In Revelation 21, we see this future revealed: a world without sorrow, without death, where God dwells with humanity. There, the workshop will become the finished sanctuary.

Why did God create the Earth? To host His image-bearers. Why did He cleanse it in the Flood? To preserve the possibility of redemption. Why will He recreate it again? Because the work He began will be completed in glory. Earth is not a meaningless pitstop—it is a proving ground, a sculptor's studio, a holy workshop.

In the hands of the Master Craftsman, we are the workmanship. What He begins, He finishes.

Prayer as a Power Outlet

If there's one thing I'm still learning, it's that prayer isn't about getting the words right. It's about staying plugged in. I used to treat prayer like a last-ditch effort—something I'd reach for in times of trouble, hoping God would hear me if I just said it the right way. But over the years, and through a lot of grace, I've begun to see it differently.

Now, I think of prayer as plugging into a power outlet. The electricity—God's presence and strength—is already there. Constant. Steady. Abundant. But unless I take the time to connect, that power can't flow into my life. And when I don't pray—when I try to manage everything with my own strength—I start to feel the power drain pretty quickly.

Looking back, I realize there were seasons when I was spiritually tired and frustrated—not because God was far away, but because I hadn't made the effort to "plug in." It's like sitting next to an outlet with a dead phone and wondering why it won't charge. The power was available. I just hadn't made the connection.

The turning point came when I stopped seeing prayer as a performance and started seeing it as a relationship. When I pray now, I'm not delivering a speech—I'm entering a conversation. Sometimes I talk, sometimes I listen. For example, every morning I start with a simple practice: I set a five-minute timer and sit in silence. I ask God to calm my thoughts and speak into the noise. Some mornings, I get clarity about His direction for that day. It's a small act of surrender that sets the tone for everything else.

I believe with all my heart that "God draws near to those who draw near to Him." James 4:8 isn't just a verse—it's a promise I've experienced firsthand. The more I converse with Jesus, the more I realize that God isn't distant. He's present. He wants to hear from me, to speak into my life, and to fill me with peace and direction—even when life feels uncertain.

Prayer doesn't always change my circumstances. But it constantly changes something in me. It centers me. It softens me. It gives me strength I didn't have and hope I didn't expect. Just as a fully charged device is ready to be used, staying connected through prayer prepares me to face the day with a heart that's open and grounded in Him.

I wish I could stay connected more often. I get distracted. I try to go it alone. But whenever I return—whenever I plug back in—I find that the power was never gone. God never moved. He was always waiting.

And that quiet truth—that His power is still flowing, and His presence still near—is something I never want to take for granted.

Faith as a Flickering Flame

"Lord, I believe; help my unbelief." That verse from Mark 9:24 has stayed with me over the years. It's one of those lines I keep returning to—not because it's dramatic or poetic, but because it's honest. It captures the tension I feel most days: I do believe, and yet, my faith wavers more than I'd like to admit.

Faith, at least in my experience, isn't a constant blaze. It's more like a flame that flickers—sometimes steady, other times sputtering. I trust in Christ. I believe in His promises. But my focus is often fractured. I try to start each day with five minutes of meditation to connect, listen, and receive my daily instruction. However, I spend most of this precious time distracted—  thinking about my schedule, something I forgot to do, or whatever's in the news. By the time I settle in, the five minutes are nearly gone. Rather than feeling refreshed, I often feel guilty for shortchanging my Shepherd.

And yet—I keep coming back. Not because I've mastered some spiritual techniques but because I know Jesus understands. He also lived in a world full of distractions. He saw firsthand how difficult it was for his disciples and followers to stay focused and centered. Moreover, He never had preconditions for strangers before meeting or healing them. That's encouraging.

Still, there are moments when doubt tries to corrupt my faith. It has never upended my faith in God, but it often disrupts my ability to stay focused on

His Son—much like Peter, who took a few steps on the water before sinking after he took his eyes off my beloved Master.

Jesus is also very familiar with Satan's tactics. The enemy knows how to use deception quite effectively. Enemy forces try to convince me that unless my faith is strong and consistent, I won't accomplish anything worthwhile. That if I can't keep the fire burning bright, I won't produce the kind of fruit that pleases God.

But that's not how Jesus responded to the man in Mark 9 who declared his unbelief. He accepted him for admitting his struggle. He helped him. That's important to remember. Faith isn't measured by volume, emotion, or radiance—it's about direction. If I'm turning toward Christ, even with a shaky hand or flickering faith, that is all that matters to Him.

There's always the temptation to settle for safe, lukewarm faith that straddles the fence between God and this world. But I don't want that either. The apostle John harshly rebuked the church in Laodicea for being lukewarm. I'd rather offer a weak flickering flame than fake intensity. So, each morning, I bring what I have. Sometimes, it's steady; other times, it's barely glowing. Either way, I trust that Jesus sees it and meets me there, as He always does.

Holy Spirit as My Conscience

When I met Jesus in 1977 during my Road to Damascus experience, I didn't fully grasp the magnitude of what had happened. But Jesus, in His wisdom, knew exactly what I needed. He sent the Holy Spirit to dwell within me—not as a distant presence, but as my counselor, guide, and voice of conviction.

Over the decades, the Holy Spirit has worked patiently and relentlessly to transform me—chiseling away at my old self through trials, discipline, and difficult lessons that pulled me from the bleachers onto the field of discipleship.

Transformation is rarely easy. There have been seasons of deep stress and personal struggle—times when I wrestled with what God was doing in me. But through it all, the Holy Spirit remained a steady presence. He revealed that the discomfort wasn't punishment, but preparation. He was forming me into the man God desires—into a disciple not just in name, but in function.

My "dirty fingernail" Jesus isn't a detached commander; He walks among us. He gets His hands and fingernails dirty. He bears burdens alongside His people. And like Jesus, the Holy Spirit has never coerced me into obedience. He has been patient, allowing detours, doubts, and failures. He's given me space to learn—never abandoning me in my weakness but using each misstep to guide me forward.

I've often kicked against the goad—the shepherd's tool meant to redirect the wandering sheep. Out of stubbornness or trepidation, I've resisted His promptings. But the Spirit never lashed back. He corrected without condemnation, always whispering truth, always drawing me back. Over time, His voice moved from occasional interruption to constant companion. He became not just a guide, but my conscience.

This inner voice compels me toward righteousness. He convicts me when I drift, but never with shame. He shapes me with grace. He helps me emit the aroma of Christ—the evidence of a life aligned with the fruits of the Spirit and pleasing to the Father.

This journey is not about achieving perfection. It's about surrendering to His transformative work daily. It's about becoming—not just someone who knows truth, but someone who lives it. And as I continue that journey, the Holy Spirit remains within me: my conscience, my compass, and my firm but gentle guide—leading me ever closer to the light and away from the shadows.

Heritage as a Living Vow

"For thou, O God, hast heard my vows: thou hast given me the **heritage** of those that **fear** thy name." Psalm 61:5

I don't speak as someone who has arrived. I haven't lived a life marked by unwavering humility or perfect surrender. If anything, I'm still learning what it means to live a life shaped by faith. But over time, I've come to realize I've been given a **heritage**—not one of position or pedigree, but of spirit—a heritage shared by those who fear God. I didn't choose it, and I haven't always honored it, but it's mine nonetheless. And I'm learning to treasure it.

That word **fear** can be confusing. We usually associate it with threat or danger, something to escape. But the fear of God—at least as I've come to understand it—isn't rooted in anxiety. It's rooted in awe. It's the overwhelming, humbling recognition of God's majesty, mercy, and presence. Not an adverse reaction to pain or suffering, but a profoundly positive response to God.

I've known fear in its raw, physical form. As a combat veteran, I've felt that cold rush in the pit of my stomach—the kind that sharpens your instincts and strips away illusion. That kind of fear is all about survival. It teaches you that life is fragile, that control is an illusion, and that death can come in an instant. But that fear fades. It passes with the moment.

The fear of God doesn't pass. It grows. Not because He becomes more threatening, but because I begin to see more clearly how vast, good, and just He is. That kind of fear doesn't drive me away; it draws me in. It steadies me, not with dread, but with reverence. It makes me want to live differently—not to avoid punishment, but to honor the One who is worthy.

Scripture makes this contrast clear: "Fear not them which kill the body but are not able to kill the soul: but rather fear him which is able to destroy both soul and body in hell." (Matthew 10:28, KJV). That's not a threat—it's a reminder of what truly matters. Earthly fears come and go. The fear of God orients the soul.

And that brings me back to heritage. The people I most admire—those I now see as spiritual ancestors—didn't just talk about God. They lived with a quiet, steady awareness of Him. Their lives weren't flashy, but they had weight. They walked humbly, trusted deeply, and bore a kind of sacred gravity. That's the heritage I've been given: to walk in the footsteps of those who lived with reverent awe.

I may never fully live up to that legacy, but I can honor it. I can continue to learn to walk in fear—not fear of harm, but fear born of wonder. And if someday someone glimpses that same reverence in me, it won't be because I claimed it. It'll be because I was claimed by it.

Fear as in His Awesomeness

There are moments when I try to imagine God the Father—His form, His face, His voice. But the more I try, the more impossible it becomes. It's like staring into the sun with the naked eye. The intensity is too great. The light is too bright. The holiness is too pure for my limited senses to grasp. And maybe that's the point.

The Bible tells us that no one can see God and live (Exodus 33:20). His presence is not just powerful— it is overpowering. Isaiah, a prophet of God, cried out, "Woe is me! for I am undone" (Isaiah 6:5) when he merely glimpsed the Lord in a vision. Even the seraphim—angels who dwell near His throne—cover their faces in His presence, crying "Holy, holy, holy" without ceasing (Isaiah 6:2-3). According to the Book of Enoch, even the archangels fear to approach the throne directly, trembling before His glory. That's not fear born of threat. That's fear born of awe.

This is what I mean when I speak of the fear of God—not the dread of punishment, but the reverent shock of encountering absolute power and holiness. It's the fear you feel when you stand on the edge of a vast canyon or stare at a night sky full of stars. You're not in danger, necessarily, but you suddenly realize how small you are—and how immense the universe is. Now multiply that feeling by infinity, and you might begin to approach what it means to fear God.

And yet, God—this untouchable, unseeable, overwhelming Being—chose to make Himself known to us. Not in His full radiance, which we could never survive, but in the person of Jesus Christ. In Him, God stepped into flesh. As Paul wrote, "For in Him dwelleth all the fullness of the Godhead bodily" (Colossians 2:9). Jesus is, in a way, the lens through which we can safely behold the light of God. He is the face we can look upon, the voice we can understand, the presence we can draw near to without being undone.

And the Holy Spirit—He is our guide. Our counselor. He doesn't just teach us about God; He prepares us to live in God's presence. Maybe He acts like a divine filter, forming in us a capacity to draw near without being scorched by the flame.

The deeper I go into this mystery, the more I sense that I'm not supposed to fully "get it." I am meant to revere it. To stand in wonder. To feel small, yes—but also grateful. Because the God who cannot be looked upon has chosen to look upon me. And not with judgment, but with love.

So, when I say I fear God, I mean I stand in awe. I tremble—not in terror, but in worship. And I thank Him that in His mercy, He has given me Jesus to behold and the Spirit to guide—lest I be blinded by glory, and still never see.

Duality as a Spiritual Principle

For decades, I wrestled with Scripture. Not its authority, but its apparent contradictions. One verse would declare that God does not change (Malachi 3:6). At the same time, another would show Him relenting or repenting (Genesis 6:6, Jonah 3:10). Jesus says His yoke is easy (Matthew 11:30) yet also warns that following Him requires taking up a cross (Luke 14:27). Paul insists we are saved by grace, not works (Ephesians 2:8–9), while James insists faith without works is dead (James 2:17). These weren't minor tensions—they were theological fault lines that made me question whether I was missing something fundamental.

Then, without fanfare, the Holy Spirit introduced me to the spiritual principle of duality, not as a philosophical abstraction, but as a divine pattern woven throughout Scripture. Suddenly, the contradictions weren't contradictions—they were complements. Scripture wasn't confusing. I was reading it flatly, expecting one-dimensional clarity from a multidimensional revelation.

Duality is everywhere in the Word of God. Scripture juxtaposes the seen and the unseen (2 Corinthians 4:18), reminding me that what's visible is temporary, and what's invisible is eternal. It affirms the dual nature of humanity— body and spirit—formed from dust yet animated by divine breath (Genesis 2:7).

Duality presents the cosmic reality of heaven and Earth, not as separate domains but as overlapping realms destined to be united (Revelation 21:1–2). It speaks of physical death and spiritual life, where dying can mean awakening (John 11:25–26). And most profoundly, it reveals the dual nature of my Lord Jesus—fully human, fully divine—walking dusty roads while bearing the weight of eternity.

This principle didn't just help me interpret Scripture. It helped me analyze the world. I began to see that what unfolds in the headlines—wars, famines, political upheaval—is not just geopolitical chaos but spiritual tremors. Earthly kingdoms rise and fall, but they echo a deeper battle between light and darkness. The visible is real, but it's not the whole story.

Duality also reframed my spiritual journey. I am both flesh and spirit, both broken and redeemed. My failures don't negate my salvation, and my suffering doesn't contradict God's goodness. They coexist. They refine. They reveal. The tension is not a flaw—it's a feature of spiritual formation.

I no longer demand that Scripture resolve itself into neat categories. I let it speak in layers. I let paradox breathe. I trust that divine truth often comes in pairs—justice and mercy, law and grace, suffering and glory. The Spirit didn't give me a system; He gave me a lens. And through that lens, I see no contradiction, but coherence. It's how the eternal speaks into the temporal.

Sin as Scars

Sin is not just something I do; it's part of who I am. It's in my DNA. Scripture says, "sin came into the world through one man, and death through sin, and so death spread to all men because all sinned" (Romans 5:12). I don't sin only because I make bad decisions—I sin because I'm born into a condition bent toward rebellion. That's not an excuse; it's reality.

When I look back on my life, my scars remind me of wounds—some self-inflicted, others caused by people who hurt me, all rooted in sin's brokenness. Today, I don't see open wounds anymore. The physical ones healed naturally, but emotional scars heal only when I seek help from my Great Physician, Jesus, and my Counselor, the Holy Spirit.

Jesus understands scars because He has them. After His resurrection, He could have returned flawless, but He chose to keep the scars in His hands and side (John 20:24-29). Thomas doubted and said, "Unless I see the nail marks in His hands and put my finger where the nails were, and put my hand into His side, I will not  believe." Jesus responded by showing His wounds. I have moments like Thomas, too, but the closer I draw to Christ, the more doubt fades. In this life, I will never be sin-free, but for Him, I try.

Unconfessed sin is like an untreated wound—it festers and worsens (Proverbs 28:13). Confessing them in prayer initiates the healing process (1

John 1:9). Healing takes time and often leaves scars. But scars have value because they tell the truth: I've been broken, but I've also been healed.

Jesus wears His scars not just to prove His identity but to show that pain, once redeemed, becomes evidence of God's victory. Redemption doesn't erase suffering; it transforms it. Like Him, I now wear my scars not as shameful reminders but as testimonies of the One who erases sin and heals me daily.

Scars also create a connection. People don't relate to perfection; they relate to honesty. When I share my failures and how God met me there, people often listen because they are curious about my story. My scars show I've been knocked down but not abandoned (2 Corinthians 4:7-9). They point to the God who heals, restores, and forgives.

I don't share to glorify sin or failure, but to glorify Jesus, who redeems both. My humanity isn't a barrier to faith; it's the place where grace is displayed (2 Corinthians 12:9). To me, every scar is a visible reminder of His mercy and power.

So, I move forward openly—not hiding, not boasting, simply acknowledging that while sin may be part of my human nature, it doesn't define my identity. My identity now is in Christ. Because of Him, my scars aren't weaknesses to hide—they're credentials of grace.

Thunder as Power

There's a saying among aviators—perhaps whispered more than spoken—that when you fly high enough, you "reach out and touch the face of God." I've always loved this maxim because I've witnessed its truth. With nearly 4,000 hours in the air—most of them strapped into the cockpit of an F-4 Phantom—I was blessed with moments that I struggle to describe.

One of those sacred memories is dancing with thunderclouds. On solo test flights above the Arizona desert, I'd sometimes find myself with enough fuel to explore those towering cathedrals of vapor. They would rise, billow, and flash—living monuments of moisture and fire. Twisting into them was like spiraling toward the gates of glory, surrounded by columns no human could ever construct, each one humming with electricity and mystery. I wasn't reckless—I was reverent. And in those moments, I wasn't just a pilot. I was a witness.

Today, a single verse brought all that back. Job 26:14: "These are but the outer fringes of His works; how faint the whisper we hear of Him! Who then can understand the thunder of His power?" (Job 26:14, NIV)

I'll admit—Job isn't a book I rush toward. Some chapters feel long and dry, and I find myself drifting toward the familiar comfort of the Gospels. But now and then, the Spirit nudges me back toward what I would've skipped. And today, in that ancient text, a thunderclap of truth found me.

"The outer fringes" zapped me. After everything I've seen—from sonic booms splitting the sky to lightning veins dancing just outside my canopy—I still realize I've only brushed the hem of His garment. I've heard the faint whisper, but never the full thunder of His power.

Even the clouds I flew through are only echoes—soft shadows—of what His true glory must be. Like a tower built of vapor, the thunderhead is real but fleeting. Its strength hints at a deeper foundation, one not made of water and wind, but of eternity and might. And I, just a man in a machine, was granted a glimpse. Not because I earned it, but because He delights to reveal Himself in slivers.

And yet, the most incredible awe comes not from knowing how small I am, but from knowing how beloved I am. Despite my limited understanding, I've been offered the hope that one day, in His Kingdom, I'll know Him as He is. Not just whispers. Not just fringes. His thunder in clarity and peace without trembling.

As a disciple of Jesus in His heavenly kingdom, I will have the opportunity to fully experience God our Father's omnipotence throughout eternity when (not if) I successfully finish traversing Jesus' righteous path while I am still on Earth.

Me as Very Special

I've walked with Jesus for four decades—stumbling, growing, questioning, and slowly drawing closer to Him. I've never had a perfect 10.0 day in service to Him—not even close. Yet lately, the Spirit has been whispering something unexpected: God is pleased with me and has something very special in mind for me.

Not just "special" in the general sense we use for all believers—justified, adopted, and welcomed into His family—but very special. At first, I thought I misheard. Me? Very special?

I've always considered myself an average Christian, grateful just to be called His. "Very special" sounded like a description for someone else—Paul, Moses, or maybe a quiet saint who prays through the night for strangers. Certainly not me.

But today something shifted. I finally believed it—not just intellectually, but deep down. I remembered a verse I marked years ago in my well-worn Bible: "What no eye has seen, nor ear heard, nor the heart of man conceived, what God has prepared for those who love him." (1 Corinthians 2:9) Beside this well-highlighted and underlined verse, I had once scribbled one small word: me.

I've read that verse many times, but today it leapt off the page. The Spirit spoke louder than usual, saying that despite my shortcomings, my love for Jesus sends a pleasing aroma to His Father. He also whispered that God has prepared something exciting for my next assignment. He withheld any details but assured me I would be pleased. That piqued my curiosity. Then came another whisper: "You're not the only one. Others are very special to Him, too."

I'll admit, my first reaction took some of the shine off the word very. If I'm one of many, how special can I be? That's when Jesus gave me a vivid mental image: He was gently holding a black sheep among a flock of white sheep. I was that black sheep—content yet distinct. Unique. Known. Loved. That image made me tear up. It was His way of saying, "Yes, you're part of the flock, but I know you. You're not lost in the crowd. And yes, I have a mission designed precisely for the unique skills the Father has given you."

I thanked Him humbly, telling Him I understood—at least in part.

Even though I see through a glass darkly, I know that being part of His team is very special because He chose me as I am—flawed—and is preparing something beyond my comprehension. Perhaps that's what "very special" really means—not that I stand above others, but that I am fully seen and still chosen. This changes how I see myself, and maybe how I treat others, knowing He sees them the same way. Indeed, this would be a very special blessing from God.

Kingdom of Heaven as a Vineyard

When I was ten years old, playing Little League baseball, my uncle, the coach, rarely let me play—except for warming the bench. I remember watching others take the field while I waited, hoping for a chance to prove myself. This benching reoccurred many times in my youth. Consequently, I know what it feels like to be unsure if I'll ever be called.

When I contemplate the parable of the laborers in the vineyard (Matthew 20:1-16), I imagine myself standing in the marketplace, wondering if anyone would choose me. That's why this vineyard owner is the kind of man I would like to work for.

I envision this vineyard owner's son stepping out early in the morning, scanning for willing hands. Those chosen at dawn head off to work immediately. Others linger in hope that there might still be work for them, and they are not disappointed. The owner continues hiring throughout the day—even taking on a final group at the eleventh hour, when only a single hour of light remains.

When it is time for payment, every worker, regardless of when hired, receives the same wage. I am sympathetic to the complaints of those who bore the day's burden. I sense their rising anger: "Shouldn't we earn more than the ones who barely worked?" But then I hear the owner's calm reply: "Friend, I am not being unfair to you... Don't I have the right to do what I want with my own money? Or are you envious because I am generous?" (Matthew 20:13,15).

My first thought is that the owner should have balanced his generosity with fairness. When I work hard, it feels natural to expect extra credit for my labor. Yet at other times, I feel like the latecomer, grateful simply to be welcomed in at all. I was thirty when I stepped into that vineyard—successful in the eyes of the world as a highly decorated fighter pilot but running on an empty spiritual tank. I brought no record of steady devotion, no résumé of spiritual success, just a worn heart and willing hands. Yet Jesus met me with the same grace as those who had served from childhood. That truth humbles me.

Even now, I sometimes slip into comparison, glancing sideways at others who seem to accomplish more, to give more, to stay longer in the field. I wonder if my labor counts the same. Then I remember the thief on the cross who had no time left, no service to point to, only a plea: "Jesus, remember me when You come into Your kingdom" (Luke 23:42). And He answered, "Today you will be with Me in paradise" (Luke 23:43). If there was room for him, there would be room for anyone willing to say yes, even at the final breath.

When I look back, I'm thankful I said yes to Jesus' offer to work on His team. I came late, but He let me in. In His Father's vineyard, there are no second-class workers, no grudging rewards—only the fullness of God's grace, freely given to every willing heart. The Kingdom of Heaven is a vineyard where all are welcomed and valued, regardless of the task or the hour of arrival.

Resurrection as from Death

The central claim of Christianity—that Jesus rose from the dead—is not just a theological concept. It's the cornerstone on which everything else depends. Without it, the rest of the story collapses.

His resurrection wasn't simply a dramatic finale; it was proof of His purpose—to defeat death and validate His identity, His mission, and His intimate relationship with the Father and the Holy Spirit—three distinct persons, yet mysteriously one.

If Jesus had not risen, He would have been just another prophet with good teachings and a tragic ending. He did rise, and I am convinced it's true. Why? Because I have come to know Him personally as my King, mentor, and friend. To non-believing friends, that sounds strange. It used to sound odd to me, too, until it didn't.

What strikes me lately is that Jesus didn't just raise Himself. He raised others—Lazarus (John 11), the widow's son in Nain (Luke 7), Jairus's daughter (Mark 5). These weren't symbolic gestures; they were real people with real families, pulled back from death's grip. And it didn't stop with Him. Through the power of the Holy Spirit, His disciples did the same. Peter raised Tabitha (Acts 9). Paul raised Eutychus (Acts 20). The Spirit didn't retire after Pentecost—it kept working through ordinary people.

In combat, I saw plenty of death, but I have never known anyone to be physically resurrected. Yet I've seen miracles—some small, some remarkable, some simply unexplainable. During my conversion, I prayed over a dead bamboo plant on my porch. The next morning, it had sprouted leaves. Coincidence? Maybe. But to me, it was a quiet echo of resurrection—a whisper that life can return where death once ruled.

More importantly, I've seen the spiritual dead come to life. That happened to me. I've seen addictions broken, bitterness softened, and hearts turned toward God. Being "born again" isn't just a metaphor—it's a transfer of ownership, a move from the dominion of darkness into the kingdom of light, from being ruled by the world to being claimed by God's Son.

Jesus' resurrection wasn't just a one-time event—it was a prototype. It showed me what's possible not just in the future resurrection of the body, but in the present resurrection of the soul. It's why I believe death doesn't get the final word—not in me, and not in those I love.

That may be the real miracle: the King of Creation didn't just defeat death for Himself but opened the door for anyone willing to step into His light. Resurrection isn't just a doctrine—it's a daily reality. It's in a bamboo tree sprouting on a porch. It's in the addict finding freedom. It's in the skeptic learning to pray. It's in me.

Humility as in Less of Myself

When I think of humility, I often associate it with being weak or meek. My first instinct is resistance, as weak implies feebleness or victimhood, such as being stepped on or shrinking back when the world demands assertion.

Even the word meek, as used in the Sermon on the Mount, has never stirred my motivation. "The meek shall inherit the earth," Jesus said. It's Scripture, and I believe it—but I confess I've never wanted to be meek. Not in the way I thought meekness was supposed to look.

But I've been rethinking humility. Not as a weakness, but as less of myself. Not in the sense of self-erasure, but in a kind of holy subtraction—a deliberate stepping aside so that Christ can be more clearly seen in me. In other words, more of him and less of me.

There's something about calling Jesus "my dirty fingernail King" that brings this deliberate depreciation into focus. I mean the Jesus who was born in the barn, not a palace.

The Jesus who washed other people's feet, who touched what was untouchable, who looked both the privileged and the powerless in the eye and said what needed to be said. The same Jesus who, though He had every right to divine immunity, allowed Himself to be humiliated—stripped, spat on, and crucified—because that was the way to win me.

Washing feet is not a weakness. That's a strength I can barely fathom. And it calls something out of me—not ambition, not striving—but a surrender like calling a truce or a ceasefire. Less of me. Not because I hate myself, but because I've come to trust that He's better at this life than I am.

There are days when I start by trying to handle everything—work, writing, strategy, relationships—with the full force of my intellect and willpower. And without fail, those days leave me feeling frayed. But when I begin the day with a quiet inner "less of me"—when I ask Christ to interrupt my assumptions, to hollow out my self-sufficiency just enough for His Spirit to breathe—it changes the day's dynamic. I act slower but love faster. I speak less but hear more. I carry less and somehow bear more fruit.

Humility like that doesn't look meek. It looks free. It looks like trusting the weight of the world to shoulders broader than mine. It seems like being small in the best way—not insignificant but willingly yoked to a King who stooped low to lift me up and upward.

So, I'm learning that humility isn't about being less for the sake of shame. It's being less for the sake of glory. Not mine—His.

Evolution as in The Bible Itself

When most people hear "evolution," they think of Darwin, fossils, and biology textbooks. But Scripture presents its kind of evolution—not about species, but about revelation, relationship, and refinement. I now see the Bible not as a static rulebook dropped from the sky but as a living narrative unfolding across centuries.

The Old Testament begins with creation but moves through covenant, law, exile, and restoration. God's relationship with humanity shifts—from walking with Adam in the garden to speaking through prophets and kings to refining His people in exile. The laws given to Moses weren't the final word; they were milestones in an ongoing process. Even within the Hebrew Scriptures, we see a growing understanding: the Psalms grapple with suffering, Ecclesiastes questions the meaning of life, and Job challenges assumptions about justice.

The New Testament brings a dramatic shift. Jesus doesn't discard the old; He fulfills it and reframes it. "You have heard it said... but I say to you..." The law moves from external compliance to internal transformation. The temple shifts from stone to Spirit. God's chosen people expand from one nation to all nations.

Even the apostles evolve. Peter moves from denying Christ to leading the church. Paul transitions from persecutor to theologian. Their letters reflect a growing understanding of grace, community, and eternity. Revelation culminates not simply in prophecy but in perspective. It doesn't return us to Eden; it unveils a new creation.

What's striking is that Scripture doesn't hide its development. It includes genealogies, revisions, and tensions—not to confuse, but to invite deeper engagement. Written over 1,500 years in Hebrew, Aramaic, and Greek, it was copied, translated, debated, and compiled—human hands at work under divine guidance. The Old Testament took shape by the 5th century BCE, and the New Testament canon was finalized in 397 AD at the Council of Carthage. This slow shaping is not a flaw; it is a feature.

I used to think faith required absolute certainty. Now I see it involves trust—clarity that often comes through process. Scripture evolves because people do. God meets us where we are, but He doesn't leave us there. From Genesis to Revelation, the story is one of movement—creation, fall, redemption, renewal.

Now, when I read the Bible, I don't just look for answers; I look for a trajectory. I trace how God's voice echoes through changing contexts yet remains consistent. That's not just divine inspiration; it's divine patience. And like the apostles who followed Jesus, I am invited to step beyond what is familiar into something deeper. The story continues—and I am part of it.

Far as East From West

There's a verse I've always found both comforting and curious: "As far as the east is from the west, so far has He removed our transgressions from us" (Ps. 103:12). It's poetic, yes—but also geometrically clever. East and West never meet. You can travel east forever and never arrive at the west. That's the point, I suppose. God's mercy doesn't just cover— it separates. It puts distance between us and our guilt that can't be measured or reversed.

Isaiah echoes this with a declaration: "I am He who blots out your transgressions for My own sake, and I will not remember your sins" (Isa. 43:25). Hebrews doubles down: "Their sins and lawless acts I will remember no more" (Heb. 8:12; 10:17). These verses are quoted as proof that God forgets our sins. But I don't think that's quite right. God doesn't forget like we forget where we left our keys. He chooses not to hold our sins against us. That's mercy—not amnesia.

Scripture clearly states that every sin that I have ever committed will eventually be revealed and evaluated. "We must all appear before the judgment seat of Christ" (2 Cor. 5:10). "The dead were judged according to what they had done as recorded in the books" (Rev. 20:12). So, which is it? Are our sins forgotten or reviewed? I think the answer lies in how God handles memory. Forgiveness isn't erasure—it's transformation. The record may remain, but the verdict changes. The wounds stay, but they no longer bleed.

Jesus didn't come back from the grave flawless. He came back wounded. "See my hands and my feet," He told Thomas (Jn. 20:27). The marks weren't erased—they were glorified. Even in Revelation, He appears as "a Lamb... as though it had been slain" (Rev. 5:6). That's not divine forgetfulness. That's divine remembrance with purpose.

I've wounds: some physical, some spiritual. I don't pretend they're gone. But I've learned they don't define me. They can testify if I let them. They can point to grace. Maybe that's what God does with our sins. He does not erase but redeems them. He does not forget but refuses to hold them against me. Father God no longer remembers them as transgressions, but as speed bumps on the road toward redemption in His Beloved Son, Jesus.

So, when I read "as far as east is from west," I don't imagine a blank slate. I envision a forgiven one like a long road littered with potholes that loving hands have filled in. A life that is still marked by choices but no longer condemned by them. God now retells my sinful storyline through the lens of mercy.

That's the kind of forgiveness that is a blessing that is overwhelming, that grows the more I think about its magnitude. It's not the kind of forgiveness that pretends nothing happened, but the kind that says: "Yes, it did. And yes, you're still mine."

Bible as a Paradox

I've come to accept a hard truth: the Bible doesn't flatter my instincts—it dismantles them. It feels like God handed me a spiritual manual that begins, "Step one: Unlearn everything you thought made sense." I now see Scripture as revealing two contradictory standards: life as a disciple of Jesus or life as a rebellious son of this world.

Take this gem: "It is more blessed to give than to receive" (Acts 20:35). My instincts argued the opposite. I spent years perfecting the art of receiving—birthday gifts, applause, even free samples at Costco. Generosity felt optional, not essential. Yet Jesus insists that giving enriches life more than hoarding. He teaches that an open hand carries more treasure than one clenched around what's "mine."

Then there's "The Son of Man came not to be served but to serve" (Mark 10:45). For many years, I admired the corner-office executive with the NASA-designed chair and a parking space that glowed like holy ground. Yet Jesus chose a basin and a towel instead of a throne, washing the feet of no one else who wanted to touch them. Somehow, this servant-king insists greatness begins in humility—and I know He's right.

Or "Better a little with righteousness than much gain with injustice" (Proverbs 16:8). C'mon, Lord, have You seen how dazzling "much gain" looks on Wall Street? Yet heaven's economy doesn't run on stock portfolios. It measures wealth by integrity and generosity—currencies that never lose value even when markets crash. That's why I'm learning to store treasures in heaven.

Then there's "Whoever wants to save their life will lose it, but whoever loses their life for me will find it" (Matthew 16:25). Before Christ, I lived for self-preservation—guarding my image, chasing success, and staying in control. Yet Jesus says true life starts when I stop clinging to it. I've learned that surrender, not self-promotion, is where life actually begins.

Finally, "It is better to be rebuked by the wise than praised by fools" (Ecclesiastes 7:5). Ouch. I like applause—it feels good, even when it comes from people who barely know me. But Scripture reminds me that correction from a wise friend is worth far more than shallow approval. Truth stings but heals; flattery tastes sweet but spoils.

The Bible is a masterclass in divine contradiction. It tells me mourning can lead to joy (Ecclesiastes 7:2–3), weakness can become strength (2 Corinthians 12:10), and being last might just put you first (Matthew 20:16). It's not mocking me—it's rescuing me from myself.

So yes, Scripture is counterintuitive. And thank God for that. If it merely echoed my instincts, I'd still be chasing comfort, applause, and control—things that rust, fade, and disappoint. Instead, it invites me into a kingdom where paradox opens the door to truth.

Apostles as Role Models

Before I accepted the Bible as truth, I needed more than tradition or emotion—I needed evidence. Especially when it came to Jesus' words recorded in the four Gospels. I approached them with skepticism, not cynicism, and asked: Who were these men who claimed to have walked with Him?

To find out, I traveled to Israel. I walked the roads of Galilee and traced the steps from the Mount of Olives to the Garden of Gethsemane. That journey gave me more than historical context—it gave me a personal connection to the Gospel writers themselves: Matthew, Mark, Luke, and John. As I studied their lives and writings, I began to see them not merely as chroniclers of Jesus' story but as role models in their own right.

Matthew became my first role model. Once a tax collector—despised by his own people—he was an unlikely choice. Yet Jesus saw potential where others saw corruption. Matthew's Gospel is orderly and analytical, built on Old Testament prophecy and structured logic. He reminds me that Jesus chooses people not for who they are, but for what He can make them.

Mark shows a different strength. His Gospel is brief and urgent, often using the word "immediately." He wastes no time with lengthy sermons or complex genealogies. Mark's style reminds me of the ideal fighter pilot—

precise and focused, unlike me. I respect the decisiveness and clarity that I occasionally achieve, although I have not yet mastered them.

Luke, the physician, adds another dimension I often lack: gentleness and compassion. His Gospel emphasizes women, the poor, and those that society frequently overlooks. He listens deeply and writes inclusively, with a quiet strength that doesn't seek attention. He challenges me to slow down and see people through the eyes of a healer.

John is my kindred spirit, both as a thinker and a writer. He focuses on meaning, not just events. His Gospel is poetic and deeply theological, beginning not with Bethlehem but with eternity: "In the beginning was the Word." John's intimacy with Jesus and his focus on divine love inspire me to think beyond facts and into eternal truths.

Together, these four Gospel accounts provide a comprehensive portrait of Jesus—His humanity, His divinity, His public ministry, and His private relationships. They were written decades after His death, at personal cost. They didn't just record history; they lived it—and many died for it.

Today, I view these Apostles as role models because they were flawed men transformed by Jesus. They came from different backgrounds with distinct personalities and talents, yet each faithfully carried out his mission. Their writings gave us not just good news, but the good news—the story that changed history and my life.

Failure to Act as Sin

I was trained as a warrior to believe that evil prevails when good people do nothing. Today, I see evil rising again, threatening global conflict or even civil war here at home. As a combat veteran, I know what it means to act under pressure—to move when others freeze. Proverbs 24:10 warns, "If you faint in the day of adversity, your strength is small." Faith without decisive action is hollow. Strength is not proven in comfort; it is revealed in crisis.

Before I became a Christian, it felt easy—even reasonable—to look away. The world's atrocities seemed distant, complex, and far removed from daily life. I told myself, "I didn't know." "It's not my place." "I'm just one person." Fear often disguised itself as wisdom—fear of being canceled, offending others, or stepping out of line. Deep down, I believed I was being prudent when, in truth, I was avoiding responsibility.

After I developed an abiding relationship with Christ and welcomed the indwelling of the Holy Spirit, that complacency was shattered. The Spirit no longer allows excuses to rest comfortably in my heart. Proverbs 24:11-12 confronts me directly: "Rescue those being taken away to death; hold back those staggering toward slaughter. If you say, 'We did not know,' does not He who weighs the heart perceive it?" I now understand that failure to act is not neutrality; it is consent.

Jesus continually instructs me that ignoring evil enables it. Churches and nations that refuse to act are not merely passive; they are complicit. God sees no difference between denial, delay, or begrudging obedience—all

are equally unacceptable because they reveal a heart out of alignment with His own. The sin of omission, when it involves the suffering of others, is grievous not because God is harsh but because He grieves at injustice. He places awareness of wrongdoing on our hearts. To suppress that awareness is to silence His voice.

Jesus never modeled passive faith. He acted decisively and unflinchingly in the face of evil. He cleansed the Temple with righteous fury, rebuked hardened hearts, and warned that anyone who causes "little ones" to stumble would be better off drowned with a millstone around their neck (Matthew 18:6-7). These are not metaphors to ponder—they are imperatives to obey.

Today, I believe that righteous anger is the flip side of love. His kind of love will not look away; it moves toward suffering rather than shrink back from it. I once saw getting involved as a burden, but my Lord shows me it can be an expression of His own heart in me. I remember one particular moment when I passed by someone clearly in need—until the Spirit nudged me to stop. What began as reluctance became joy as I saw His hand at work. These moments are changing me. Courage is no longer about proving my "goodness" but trusting His, allowing His love to move through me. That, I am learning, is where true strength lives.

Dreams as a Netherworld

I freely admit that I know very little about what happens during sleep—and I'm not convinced anyone else does either. Sleep experts may understand the mechanics of REM cycles and brain waves, but I suspect they know about dreams as much as marine biologists know about the deepest trenches of the ocean—just enough to be humbled by how little we know.

I think dreams represent a kind of netherworld, a spiritual intersection between the material and unseen realms. Scripture refers to the netherworld as the abode of the dead, not always a place of punishment, but a shadowy domain where souls linger and light is faint. That's how my dreams often feel: strange, disjointed, and unsettling. They don't follow the logic of waking life. They feel like echoes from somewhere else—fragments of conversations I never had or places I never visited, yet somehow eerily familiar.

Over the years, I've noticed a pattern: after days devoted to faith—seeking God's light, praying, and serving—I'm more likely to experience disturbing dreams. It's as if the principalities and powers cast out of heaven (Ephesians 6:12) take notice and retaliate. On days when I chase ordinary pursuits, my sleep is calmer. But when I focus on the things of God, nights can turn quite turbulent.

This makes sense to me. The netherworld is a contested space where spiritual forces attempt to influence, confuse, or torment.

Scripture often links spiritual conflict to the Fourth Watch (3:00–6:00 AM). It was during this watch that Jesus walked on water toward His terrified disciples, who thought they had seen a ghost (Matthew 14:25-26).

Jacob wrestled with God during these hours (Genesis 32:24–30), and Israel was delivered from Egypt at the same watch (Exodus 14:24). These accounts suggest the veil between realms may be thinnest when the world is quiet and most people are asleep.

My most bizarre dreams—violent, salacious, perplexing, and just plain weird—often come in those early morning hours. I wake up grumpy, disoriented, and spiritually fogged, feeling as if I have traveled through a strange and hostile country.

Yet God, in His mercy, has taught me to begin each day with early morning devotions. A short prayer, a few verses of Scripture, and quiet meditation are usually enough to dispel the residue of the night and reset my footing.

That doesn't mean I stay perfectly on the narrow path all day. I stumble like anyone else. But I am reminded that while the dreamworld may be chaotic and mysterious, the waking world offers clarity and renewal when we begin the day with Him. That's the grace I rely on, morning after morning.

Apostasy as a Flaming Torch

I've always been drawn to the idea of finding my way alone. There is a quiet pride in solving problems, charting paths, and trusting my instincts. Ever since leaving apostasy in my rearview mirror, my yoking with Christ has slowly replaced that go-it-alone machismo with a much different and gentler manner of manliness.

Isaiah 50:10-11 challenges me every time I read it: "Those who light their own fires and provide themselves with flaming torches will lie down in torment." That image hits home. A flaming torch may feel bold and bright, but it's fleeting and dangerous. It illuminates what I want to see, not what God knows I need.

In the darkness of life's uncertainties—job loss, broken relationships, or quiet doubts—I am tempted to reach for my torch. For me, it's late-night planning, overthinking, and trying to outsmart fear. But Isaiah's warning lingers.

My torch, though it sparks with confidence, casts shadows that distort the path. It burns hot, then fades, leaving me disoriented. By contrast, Psalm 119:105 reminds me that God's Word is "a lamp to my feet and a light to my path"—soft but steady, lighting only the next step, not the whole route.

In moments of crisis, the world tells me to lean on my understanding, exactly what Proverbs 3:5-6 warns against. My latent machismo urges me to map out solutions and then check in with Jesus as if He were a consultant. But like Jeremiah's cracked cistern (Jeremiah 17:5-8), my efforts always leak. Plans unravel, leaving me thirsting for something more. God offers what I cannot manufacture: a fountain that never runs dry and a light that never flickers.

There's a humbling clarity in John 8:12, where Jesus says, "I am the light of the world. Whoever follows me will not walk in darkness." To admit my light isn't enough is hard. My torch feels personal, crafted by my own hands, a testament to my strength. To lay it down is to confess that I am not as self-sufficient as I would like to be. Yet Psalm 18:28 whispers, "You, Lord, keep my lamp burning; my God turns my darkness into light."

Matthew 6:22-23 warns about eyes that pretend to see yet fill the body with darkness. My torch can be like that: convincing me I see clearly when I'm stumbling. The torment Isaiah describes isn't always dramatic—it can be the quiet ache of burnout or the restlessness of a wandering heart.

Apostasy as a flaming torch warns me not to fly solo in the dark without instruments. God offers His lamp, His Son's unending light, and the Holy Spirit's counsel to trust Their path. I don't need to blaze a trail. I only need to follow Their righteous way.

Salvation as a Narrow Gate

"Enter through the narrow gate. For wide is the gate and broad is the road that leads to destruction, and many enter through it. But small is the gate and narrow the road that leads to life, and only a few find it." — Matthew 7:13-14

When I read this, I don't hear Jesus warning the world—I listen to Him speaking directly to me. This isn't a general caution about unbelievers or outsiders. It's a personal directive. He's telling me that the life path is narrow, complex, and easily missed. And if I'm not careful, I'll drift toward the broad road—not because I reject Him outright, but because the broad road feels easier, safer, and more scenic.

I believe the narrow gate is not just a metaphor—it's a spiritual reality. It opens only from the inside, and only Christ can open it. I can't force it, fake it, or bypass it. I have to be changed to fit through it. That's the hard part. I prefer a path that lets me keep my comforts, my pride, my assumptions. But Jesus makes it clear: the gate is narrow, and the road is hard.

In Luke 13:24, He says, "Make every effort to enter through the narrow door, because many... will try to enter and will not be able to." That's another warning. It means effort is required—not just belief or good intentions. I have to strive. I have to examine myself. I have to stay awake spiritually. That's not the course I would choose for myself, but it's the one God has laid out.

I also take seriously what Jesus says in John 10:1: "Anyone who does not enter the sheep pen by the gate, but climbs in some other way, is a thief and a robber." That tells me there are no shortcuts. If I try to climb over the wall—through religious performance, moral self-righteousness, or spiritual pride—I'm not just mistaken. I'm an evildoer. And I will be expelled.

Jesus reinforces this truth through multiple parables—the Sower, the Ten Bridesmaids, the Talents, the Sheep and Goats. These aren't stories about outsiders. They're about believers. These people are like me, who profess faith, serve, and wait for the bridegroom. And yet, only a portion of them make it through the narrow gate. That tells me salvation is not saying "I believe in you" but "I follow You!" It's not about affiliation or intention. It's about transformation, obedience, and perseverance.

I believe the narrow gate is Christ Himself. And I must be conformed to Him—not just admire Him—to enter. That's the course I've been given. It's not easy. It's not scenic. But it's the only way that leads to life.

The good news is, I don't have to navigate this challenging course alone. If I keep my eyes fixed on Jesus, He not only shows me the way—He walks it with me.

Power as a False God

There's a strange quiet that follows the pursuit of power. Not the kind that comes from surrender or peace, but the kind that settles in after you've climbed high enough to see how the world works from the summit.

In the eyes of the world, I've been told I sit near the top — in combat, in corporate circles, in the metrics that define success. Whether that's true or not is beside the point. What matters is what I've come to see from that vantage: power, when pursued for its own sake, is a false god.

It promises control, influence, safety, and even a sense of identity. But it demands worship. It asks for your time, your relationships, and your integrity. Earthly power rarely gives back what it promises. Like the crumbling golden calf at Sinai, that was crafted from fear and impatience. Satan offers it when we don't trust God to act, when waiting feels unbearable, when surrender feels like weakness.

Satan knows this. He's been using power as bait since Eden. "You will be like God," he said — not offering intimacy, but autonomy. He tried again with Jesus in the wilderness, offering all the kingdoms of the world in exchange for worship. But Jesus didn't bite. He knew that real power isn't seized — it's received. And it's only given to those who will wield it for God's purposes, not their own.

That's the paradox. The power of this material world is counterfeit. The power the Holy Spirit offers us is real, but it comes through surrender. It's not flashy. It doesn't always look like victory. Sometimes it looks like silence, restraint, washing feet, or carrying a cross.

I've felt the tension. In moments of triumph, there's a whisper: "This is what you were made for." But it's not the voice of God. It's the voice of pride, dressed up in achievement. And in quieter moments, when I've laid down the need to be seen, to be right, to be strong — I've felt something more profound. A power that doesn't puff up but lifts. A power that doesn't dominate but is given to us for others.

Power is a false god when it becomes the goal. But when it's surrendered — when it's placed back into the hands of the Omnipotent One — it becomes a tool for glory, not self. God shares His power freely, but only with those who won't hoard it. Those who know it's not theirs to begin with.

So, I'm learning to let go. To stop measuring strength by influence or control. To prevent bowing to the golden calf of world power. And to start receiving the kind of power that flows from heaven, that is quiet, steady, holy. The kind that changes hearts, not headlines.

Righteousness as in Weariness

"Let us not grow weary in doing good, for at the proper time we will reap a harvest if we do not give up." — Galatians 6:9

Weariness is not a sin. It's a symptom of striving toward righteousness in a world that resists it. Even Jesus grew weary in doing His Father's will. He withdrew often to solitary places to pray, not out of weakness, but out of necessity. The Gethsemane is an example of utmost weariness, where sweat became blood and the weight of obedience nearly crushed the Son of God.

Paul understood this weariness. He didn't write Galatians 6:9 as a slogan. He wrote it as a man who had been beaten, jailed, shipwrecked, starved, and left for dead—all for the sake of doing good. His resume of suffering is unmatched except by Christ Himself. And yet, Paul pressed on, not because it was easy, but because he knew the reward was real. From my perspective, Paul's greatest reward wasn't earthly—it was eternal. He was beheaded for his Master, and I believe he entered glory with a crown that no Roman sword could tarnish.

Compared to Jesus and Paul, I grow weary far more easily. Weariness creeps in when fatigue, impatience, or frustration sets in. That's when the demon on my shoulder whispers doubts: "You're following a God you can't see or hear—just a figment of your imagination." But then my guardian angel counters with truth: "This life is a test. Those who endure will be rewarded."

Life's tests aren't graded on a curve. They are pass-fail. The trials we face are not random. They're diagnostic. They reveal whether we desire the eternal or the ephemeral. At the spiritual kindergarten level, the tests are simple: share, forgive, trust. But as we mature, the tests intensify. Adult faith is forged in suffering, in choosing unseen glory over visible gain.

Jesus and Paul passed their tests. They chose the light of God over the glitter of the world. That same choice lies before me. I can chase temporary rewards—prestige, power, wealth—or I can pursue eternal ones that never rust, fade, or die. For me, the decision is clear. I choose Jesus, the genuine Light, the conduit of the Father's infinite radiance.

And when I stumble, when I grow tired and ask "why," I've learned to ask my Lord for help. He doesn't scold—He lifts. Like Peter sinking in the waves, I find that as long as I keep my eyes on Him, I can walk through any storm. Every quiz, every trial, every whisper of doubt becomes an opportunity to reaffirm my choice: the eternal over the temporary, the unseen over the seen, the Light over the shadow.

So, like a weary rock climber, I struggle upward. Not because I'm strong, but because He is. And in due time, if I do not give up, I will reap a harvest as His reward.

Busyness as a Fragile Fortress

I've come to see that busyness wasn't just something that happened to me—it was something I allowed, even welcomed. It filled gaps. It gave structure. It made me feel useful, even when I wasn't entirely sure what I was aiming at. For much of my life, I chose busyness not out of ambition, but out of a quiet need to keep things moving. Stillness felt uncertain, even awkward. So, I filled the space.

Looking back, I realize that busyness helped me avoid more complex questions about identity, purpose, and sometimes, pain. It wasn't that I was running from God or the people I loved. However, the sheer momentum of activity left little room for anyone else to enter. I had unknowingly built a fortress—one that looked like discipline or responsibility from the outside, but that quietly kept people, and even God, at a distance.

My early life shaped some of this habit. A chaotic childhood and a year spent in combat taught me that stillness wasn't always safe. In those seasons, movement meant control—or at least the illusion of it. Busyness provided a rhythm that helped drown out uncertainty. But over time, what started as a coping mechanism evolved into a lifestyle. And eventually, a limitation.

Like the blind men Jesus healed, He opened my eyes to see how that nearsightedness excluded others—especially those closest to me. When every hour was accounted for, there was little margin for spontaneous

conversation, unhurried prayer, or truly seeing and hearing those around me.

Jesus moved with purpose but never in a hurry. He saw people. He stopped for them. He carved out silence to commune with His Father. And when He visited the home of Mary and Martha, He said tenderly to the anxious one: "You are worried and upset about many things, but only one thing is necessary. Mary has chosen what is better..." (Luke 10:41-42).

That line hits home. I realize now that always filling the void meant I was missing the voice that mattered most. The Holy Spirit has also been gently confronting me—not with shame, but with clarity. He's shown me that love requires room—room to listen, room to be interrupted, room to be present.

Today, I'm learning to make different choices. To create space instead of constantly filling it. To let the fortress crumble so others can come in—and so Jesus doesn't have to knock. I still value structure and movement, but I now see that some of life's most meaningful moments happen in the in-between. And it's in those moments that the fragile fortress gives way to something far more substantial: a relationship with Him.

Grace as Free, Salvation as Difficult

When I accepted the offer to enter the U.S. Air Force Academy, it came without tuition or fees. Just a signature and a commitment. But that "free" entry led to years of training, discipline, and transformation. Becoming an officer demanded everything. Becoming a combat-ready fighter pilot demanded even more. The offer was free. The arduous journey was not.

Grace, as I've come to understand it, was extended by God the Father without cost. It was His invitation—unearned, undeserved, and unconditional. But salvation? That's something different. Salvation must be pursued with resolve. It must be walked out. It must be earned—not through merit or works alone, but by faithfully following the path set forth and traveled by Jesus. Grace is not the finish line—it's enlistment. The moment marked the beginning of a life shaped by obedience, sacrifice, and perseverance. Discipleship didn't unfold passively. It required training. It required surrender. It required being broken down and rebuilt stronger.

There were seasons when I admired Jesus more than I followed Him. Times when the cross I was given felt too heavy to carry, and self-denial seemed too much to ask. The gift of grace was always there—but salvation, I've come to believe, is only truly received by those who endure. And endurance is no small thing. Conviction fades. Compromise creeps in. Spiritual drift takes hold. The temptation to coast, to be liked, to avoid the cost of faith, is part of the journey. And yet, each time I turned back to the cross, He was there—coaching, bandaging wounds, lifting me, and urging me upward.

God also gave me a quiet superpower. The Holy Spirit doesn't shout. He whispers. And salvation has felt distant when I've ignored that whisper. That still, small voice has redirected me more times than I can count—away from pride, toward humility; away from self-preservation, toward surrender; away from the world, and toward the Light. Listening is part of the training. And training is part of the transformation.

There have been moments when the enemy whispered, Was it worth it? Would you choose this path again? And the answer, without hesitation, is yes. Jesus walked with me through every valley, lifted me when I fell, and taught me what needs to be known. In that journey, a profound rapport has formed—with my Master, my Friend. God called Abraham 'friend' (James 2:23), and I believe Jesus feels the same about me. That is worth every cost.

Refinement continues. The arduous trek hasn't diminished. But the joy of knowing Him has deepened in ways I never expected. God has transformed me into an instrument He can use according to His will and purpose. The heavenly host no longer sees me as an enemy—but as a child of God. In the truest sense of the word, I have become Jesus' soulmate.

Hard Heart as a Clenched Fist

"You shall not harden your heart or shut
your hand against your poor brother."
Deuteronomy 15:7

This verse sticks in my mind. It exposes the spiritual anatomy of selfishness: a hardened heart and a clenched fist. In today's noisy, chaotic world, it's easy to overlook suffering, even among those closest to me. I've found that my heart doesn't harden all at once. It calcifies slowly, quietly, until compassion feels inconvenient and generosity feels optional.

Growing up, I believed courtesy was for strangers. Politeness was a public virtue, not a private one. That principle contributed to a growing chasm between my projected self and my true self. I could be gracious in public and guarded at home. But Jesus, even when overwhelmed by crowds and needs, never lost sight of the individual. Though He had emptied Himself of divine power—kenosis—the Holy Spirit within Him responded. When the woman touched His garment, He felt power leave Him. He didn't initiate the healing, but He noticed it. That Spirit-led sensitivity is what I long for.

James, the half-brother of Jesus, wrote with piercing clarity: "As the body without the spirit is dead, so faith without works is dead also." I've heard too many sermons that elevate faith while minimizing the necessity of good work. I've come to believe they are equal. Faith opens the door to Spirit power. Good work is faith in action. When I pick up my cross and walk with Jesus, the Holy Spirit generates good works through me that honor Him and please the Father.

Deuteronomy 15:11 doesn't suggest generosity—it commands it. "You shall open wide your hand to your brother, to the needy and the poor." Not a clenched fist. Not a reluctant offering. An open hand. A softened heart. A posture of surrender and compassion.

But the world can quickly quench the Spirit if I become overly task-oriented and emotionally guarded. I neglect to read scripture. I fail to listen to the Spirit's whisper. And so, I must return—again and again—to James and Deuteronomy. I must reread, recall, and reawaken.

As a serial business developer, I've launched many startups. In 2010, the Lord placed something profound in my heart: to help the poor in underserved communities start businesses that provide them with what they need (James 2) and the ability to be self-sufficient. He told me to do this pro bono—no money taken.

Working for free was a hard pill to swallow. But I gulped it down and planted a grassroots movement called Jobenomics. Today, it's now grown to 100 chapters on four continents, not because of me, but because of Him. When I unclenched my fist, He filled my hand, and multiplied the seed, which was exceedingly worth every second I invested in Him over the last fifteen years.

Faith & Trust as Troubled Times

I've come to believe that faith and trust aren't just spiritual ideals—they're survival tools. Not the kind you pull out when things are going well, but the kind you cling to when the ground gives way beneath you. In troubled times, faith isn't ornamental. It's structural.

Psalm 46 says, "God is our refuge and strength, an ever-present help in trouble." That phrase—ever-present—has stuck with me. It doesn't say God is occasionally available or conditionally attentive. It says He's there. Always. Even when the fig tree doesn't bud, as Habakkuk puts it. Even when the outcomes we hoped for don't materialize. That's where trust begins—not in the presence of fruit, but in the confidence that the root system runs deep.

I've had seasons where everything visible seemed to contradict what I believed. Plans unraveled. People disappointed. The storm, like in Mark 4, was real. And loud. And Jesus' question to the disciples—"Why are you so afraid? Do you still have no faith?"—felt less like a rebuke and more like a mirror. I wasn't afraid because I lacked belief in God's existence. I was fearful because I doubted His proximity. I mistook silence for absence.

But faith, as Hebrews 11:1 reminds us, is the substance of things hoped for, the evidence of things not seen. It's not blind optimism. It's spiritual infrared—seeing what natural eyes can't. Trust, then, is choosing to stay tethered to that unseen anchor. Not because the storm isn't real, but because the anchor is more real.

I've learned that trust is a thermostat, not a thermometer. Isaiah 26 says, "You will keep in perfect peace those whose minds are steadfast, because they trust in you." That peace doesn't come from the absence of trouble. It comes from a decision to adjust my internal spiritual thermostat to reduce the heat of external chaos. It's not passive. It's deliberate.

When I find myself in turbulent waters, I often picture myself stranded in a small boat in a rough sea, anchored just below the surface. This boat is battered, but it doesn't drift. The anchor isn't visible, but it holds. That's what faith feels like in troubled times. Not triumphant. Not flashy. Just steady. Waiting for my Lord and Savior to come to my aid.

I don't write this as someone who's mastered trust. I write it as someone who's learning, slowly, that faith isn't about controlling outcomes. It's about surrendering to a trustworthy God. Not because I always feel it, but because I've seen enough to know He holds when everything else breaks loose.

Troubled times don't make faith irrelevant. They make it essential. And trust isn't a feeling—it's a choice to stay tethered. Even when the fig tree doesn't bud. Even when the storm doesn't stop. Even when the silence feels heavy. Anchored in Christ, I have refuge from my distress.

www.ingramcontent.com/pod-product-compliance
Lightning Source LLC
Chambersburg PA
CBHW040815120726
48005CB00012B/1418

PREFACE

Today, we are living in the 21st century, amidst fast-developing technologies, digital economies, global uncertainty and a fast-changing geopolitical scenario. In such a turbulent environment, time is the most critical resource and it must be managed effectively. It is also important to have good speed in various actions like Reading, Writing, Thinking, Analyzing, Decision-Making, Planning and Execution. Time is a vital resource and it is limited to just 24 hours, available daily to everybody. This includes day and night, where we need 6-7 hours of sleep, 1-2 hours of commuting to the workplace, 2-3 hours with the family, 1 hour for physical exercise/ walking, 1-2 hours for having food and getting ready to go to the workplace. Thus, we get daily just 8-10 hours at the workplace. It is pertinent to note that time went past today, will not come back tomorrow. However, every tomorrow will come with new hopes, challenges and opportunities. Therefore, we must plan today for the best time utilization tomorrow.

With global connectivity through affordable and reliable internet and 5G mobile communication networks, time-zone difference has become a boon instead of a limitation. Time-zone advantage allows us to deploy our project teams globally and stay connected functionally on a 24x7 basis. Hence, we can have global business partners and can work round the clock and across the globe.

The goal of this book is to review the current state of time management techniques/strategies and suggest an approach which helps individuals and their organizations to grow fast. The book provides jargon-free, compact and easy-to-grasp material for young professionals. It aims to show them the pathway to learn newer skills continuously to grow through effective time management and provide a competitive edge to the organization. This book will also help the Presidents/Directors/CEOs of organizations to invest more in training their young professionals in time management techniques/strategies.

In today's uncertain global environment, the survival and growth of business is through fast acquiring knowledge of new skills and processes, quickly adopting new techniques and networking to share knowledge for faster growth. This book will be a handy reference/guide for students undergoing professional studies, business executives, team leaders, managers and teachers/professors. Salient points in each chapter are given in bulleted form for ready to be used as PowerPoint (PPT) slides by teachers, professors, HRD managers, and senior management.

There are many books/e-books/white papers, blogs and Google pages on time management. These are very inspiring and valuable inputs since some of these contain case studies and research work of world-famous management and technology experts/gurus. In this book, due emphasis has been given to continuous learning new skills, networking and time sharing.

To create a greater impact on the reader the book has been written in a simple language in a conversational mode as if the reader and author are having a face-to-face conversation. The book is designed to empower senior management of any organization and young professionals in any field like Engineering, IT, Business Management, Digital Marketing/Sales, Design, Production, Projects, Banking, Insurance, Education, Healthcare, Journalism, Construction and Government or Private sectors. Repetition of certain words in various sections is deliberate to reemphasize and create a deeper impact.

I have tried to add some value, based on my experience of 30 years in Telecommunications and Computer Technology, while serving in the Indian Army (Signals), 10 years in senior management in the corporate sector, 16 years as an educationist and having a long association with leading universities in the USA, UK, Australia and India.

It is recommended to treat this book as your companion and spare a little time, every day to open it and highlight a few paragraphs of your choice. Rest assured that within 45 days of picking up this book/eBook, you will become a more time-conscious professional who is more proactive, adaptable to new technologies and ensures success/growth. You will soon start balancing time for Job and Family.

Contact: Email: drsarbjit@gmail.com, Twitter (X): www. twitter.com/sarbjit_singh

LinkedIn: www.linkedin.com/in/dr-sarbjit-singh

Blog 1: https://sarbjit-knowledgeshare-success.blogspot.com

Blog 2: https://sarbjit-spirituality-godconnect.blogspot.com

– Dr. Sarbjit Singh

ACKNOWLEDGEMENTS

I am thankful of Prof Ramesh Chandra for suggesting slight change in book title. He has also suggested some additional examples for realizing true value of tine. I am also very thankful to all the experts who have very kindly spared their valuable time to go through the manuscript and provide very valuable inputs, which will inspire the readers.

I sincerely thank Dr. Nirmaljit Dhami, Director, Dept. of Neuro Science, El-Camino Hospital, Mountain View, CA, USA, for her suggestions to improve the contents of the chapter on Time and Health Relationship.

I thank Vikramjit Singh, CTO, Software Junction, India and Romy Bajaj, BRM, Permod Richard, India, for persuading me to write this book.

My sincere thanks to the publisher Notion Press and their team of experts for their valuable suggestions to improve the layout of the book for better market appeal.

I sincerely thank many Authors, Research Scholars, Economists and Technology Leaders, whose Quotations/"Thoughts", I have used freely to inspire young minds to keep going, learning newer technologies and progress.

It also gives me immense pleasure to thank my grandchildren Angad Singh Dhami, Mehr Kaur Dhami, Jaiveer Singh Dhami and Amitesh Singh, as I could not spend enough time with them but they cheerfully supported me in completing this book.

– Dr. Sarbjit Singh

REVIEW BY EXPERTS

1. The book gives guidelines as to how to plan and effectively manage our time keeping in mind a proper balance in time spent at work, in commuting and at home. The author has stressed that any postponement of investment in time today will cost us more tomorrow. Swami Vivekananda said, "A rain drop from the sky: if it is caught by clean hands, is pure enough for drinking. If it falls in the gutter, its value drops so much that it can't be used even for washing your feet. Always be associated with people who are time conscious, disciplined and achievers. You will experience your own inner transformation in respect of proper time management". A must read book.

   Dr. S.K. Aggarwal (Professor Emeritus), Former Prof & Head of Mech Engg. Dep't. PEC, Chandigarh; Former Director Technical Education, U.T. Chandigarh. Former Director Academic Punjab State Board of Technical Education & IT, Chandigarh.

2. It is well known that most people use only a fraction of their human potential during their lifetime. This is not because of external constraints, but because of the barriers and walls we ourselves build around us. Sarbjit Singh's book– *Effective Time Management* - is a comprehensive guide on how one can effectively and quite easily improve the way one works and lives. Explained in a very simple and intelligible style – the book would be an immensely useful aid to all those who wish to achieve their highest potential.

Ravi Chaudhry, Former Chairman, Companies in Tata Group; and Author - Capitalism to Peopleism: Inspiring a Leadership Transformation & Quest for Exceptional Leadership: Mirage to Reality.

3. Dr. Sarbjit Singh's book is highly applicable to everyday life. Whether, one is a professional looking to improve efficiency, a student striving for better time utilization, or someone trying to balance work and personal life. The book starts with time as a critical resource and gradually builds on key concepts such as time consciousness, job awareness, self-awareness, time distractors, time savers, relationship between time and speed, time zone advantage and personal health. Dr. Sarbjit Singh's expertise and clear writing style make it an engaging and practical guide for achieving greater productivity at workplace and joy at home. Highly recommended!

Dr. Sanjay khakhil, Professor in Computer science Engineering Department at Golgotha's College of Engineering and Technology, Greater Noida, UP, India.

4. In my long experience of corporate and education sector, I have often heard many working executives saying "I am regularly working long hours and even, taking work home, but still missing deadlines. I have no time for my family and friends." These are symptoms of poor time management and not maintaining work-life balance. Dr. Sarbjit Singh has authored a very simple and useful book in his lucid style which serves as a handy guide book for learning vey comprehensively, the time management skills as well as an excellent 'mantra' for happy work-life balance. The book is in the "must read" category for any college/university library and HRD department of any organization.

Prof. (Brig.) Ramesh Chandra. Ex-Director, Institute of Agri-business Management, Noida; Ex-Dean & Area Chairperson (HR & OB), Delhi Business School, New Delhi; Visiting Professor (HR, OB, Strategy & MDPs); Corporate Trainer & Executive Coach (Soft Skills)

5. The book by Dr. Singh concentrates on time management and balancing between a career and family. I remember a young faculty member in a university at which I was a guest Fulbright lecturer many years ago, who had notably sacrificed his family life for his career, and how our discussions eventually helped him to turn things around. I imagine this book could have done the same, if it were available then. The list of things to do and not do, given in this book are useful guides for anyone working in any field to plan better and to manage their lives. This book is an excellent guide to individuals who need to overcome their troubles with time management and balancing their career and family lives.

Dr. Saeed Niku, Emiratis Prof. Mechanical Engineering; Cal Poly. Luis Obispo, California, USA.

6. The book, by Dr. Sarbjit Singh highlights the value of Time Management in our work and family life. Time Management is in fact the essence of life. Balancing time between work, family, friends and self makes a big difference in cruising through life successfully and with honour and dignity. The book was long overdue and I highly appreciate that Dr. Sarbjit Singh has written it to help all professionals to cruise through their life cycle successfully. I hope Dr. Sarbjit Singh continues to enlighten us with more titles which help us in making our life successful.

Dr. HS Chhabra, Alumina of IIT Madras and IIM Ahmedabad, Former Professor and Dean Academics in NITIE, (Renamed as IIM Mumbai), Professor in IIM Lucknow, Professor, University of Nizwa in Oman, Professor and Dean Academics in IIM Shillong and Director, School of Management in NIT Agartala, India.

7. This book by Dr. Sarbjit Singh is a Practical Guide to Effective Time Management, which is a reflection of his real-life experiences and professional journey. Instead of just theoretical concepts, the author shares practical scenarios and personal anecdotes, making it highly relatable and easy to implement. His approach is not just about managing time but maximizing its value to achieve personal and professional success.

    Having known Dr. Sarbjit Singh for the past eight years, I can confidently say that his depth of knowledge, futuristic vision, and sharp wit make him an exceptional thinker. I highly recommend this book, especially to young professionals and students, who can gain immense insight from the author's experiences. Time is a crucial asset, and this book serves as a roadmap to utilizing it effectively for career growth and life management. A must read for anyone looking to take control of his/her time.

    Adv. Dr. Nitin Sharma , (Supreme Court of India), (Hony President), Aplomb Group of Education, New Delhi

8. Dr. Sarbjit Singh has come out with his insightful book, Effective Time Management: Key to Work- Life Balance. Indeed, it is a landmark exposition on the compelling issues as a result of prevailing global uncertainty and information deluge engulfing us. The book reviews the current state of time management techniques/strategies and suggests an approach which helps individuals and their organizations to grow fast. The book is jargon-free, easy-to-grasp material for young professionals, showing

them the pathway to learn newer skills continuously, grow through effective time management and provide a competitive edge to the organization. This book will also help the Presidents/Directors/CEOs of organizations to invest more in training their young professionals in time management techniques/strategies.

The book provides a road map to effectively evolve an appropriate strategy to balance the time both for doing the job efficiently and fulfill family responsibilities willingly. It emphasizes on need to prepare "To Do" lists, prioritize various tasks, and allocate time blocks judiciously.

Dr. Ranjit Singh (PhD, IIT Kanpur), Editor-in-Chief, AKGEC International Journal of Technology, Ghaziabad, editor_journal@akgec.ac.in 9868041558

01

INTRODUCTION

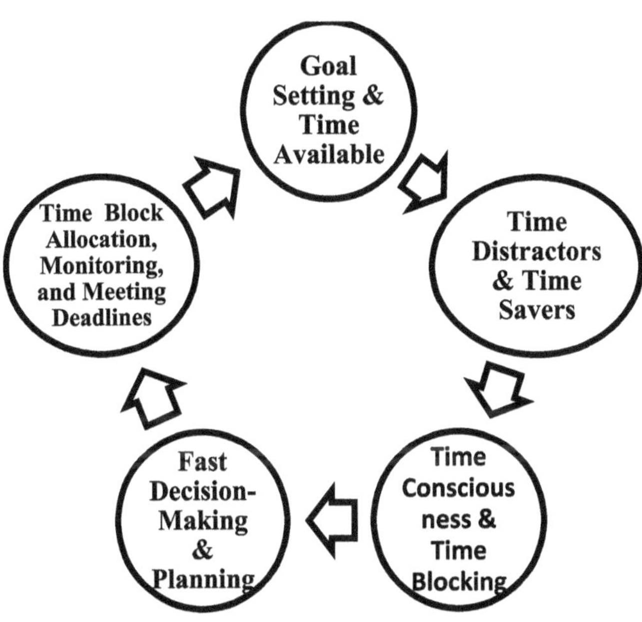

Figure 1.1 A typical Time Cycle

"Don't make the same decision twice. Spend time and thought to make a solid decision the first time so that you don't revisit the issue unnecessarily."

– Bill Gates

In today's highly uncertain and competitive market environment, time is the most critical resource for every individual and every organization/institution. Effective time management is the cornerstone for a successful career and balanced family life for any professional. Daily availability of time to everyone is limited to just 24 hours, which is related to one revolution of the earth around its axis. This rotation creates day and night conditions, depending upon the location of the earth with reference to the sun.

Out of 24 hours, time available to us to perform various duties at the workplace and at home is limited to 10 to 14 hours per day. Therefore, this available time must be well-planned and utilized effectively. It is necessary that all people at all levels, in every organization, should be time conscious and manage their time efficiently and also help others to work efficiently. The organization could be a government department, public sector company or private company. These could have various sectors like Construction (Buildings, Roads, Bridges, and Dams), Irrigation, Railways, Aviation, Road Transport, Healthcare, HRD, Education, Agriculture, Finance, Mining and Exploration, Oil and Refinery, Chemicals, Shipping, Research & Development (R&D), Space & Research and others. As an employee, one could be a Door Keeper, Security Guard, Gardner, Lift operator, Receptionist, Team Leader, Manager or a CEO in an organization. Likewise, one could be a Student, Teacher or Principal in a school/college or a professor, Head of Department (HOD), Dean or Vice Chancellor in a university or any individual professional working as a Team Leader, Sales Manager, Research Scholar, Vice president or Chairman/President. Everyone gets just 24 hours every day, which includes night-time. Likewise, family members also get just 24 hours. All should be time-conscious and cheerfully share workload/responsibilities.

Achieving right balance between work and family life is important to every professional. This entails knowing when and how much to focus on work and when and how much time to spend with loved ones or hobbies. Learning and practicing this balancing act can help us to become more proactive and stay happy throughout the days/weeks.

Success vs. Productivity. Success and productivity is not the same thing. In fact, productivity is related to the concept that if one produces more, one will sell more and gain maximum profit. On the other hand, success relates to doing a job efficiently, delivering on time and meeting user requirements fully, with no time or cost overruns.

Time Availability. [3] In normal daily life, one needs 6-8 hours of sound sleep, 1-2 hours for morning chores, one and half hour maybe for health-care exercise, like brisk walking/Yoga/meditation, and one hour to get ready, take breakfast and organize for going to the workplace. One may go to the workplace by train/metro/bus/taxi or own car and spend say 1-2 hours commuting to the workplace. Thus, net available time may be just 8-10 hours of working at one's workplace. This available 8-10 hours need to be well planned and utilized diligently to meet deadlines, as assured to various customers. However, while planning and scheduling activities, one need to give first priority to the job, second to the family/ children and last to the friends.

Importance of Time. We all know that time does not wait for anyone and it just keeps ticking and flowing away like the river water. Once the river water has flown past us, we cannot get that water back. Likewise, if time has elapsed and we did not perform the scheduled job, we cannot meet the deadline. Therefore, it is up to us to plan and harness our time to build our successful careers and also look after our families. The importance of effective time management is given in succeeding paragraphs.

At the Workplace. [5]

- **Career Advancement.** Well managed time helps us in meeting deadlines, taking on new challenges, working with full efficiency and advancing in our career.

- **Increased Productivity.** Prioritizing tasks and allocating time slots help us to focus and accomplish more in less time.

- **Reduces Stress.** Well managed time provides a structured approach which mitigates the feeling of being overwhelmed and reduces mental stress.

At Home. [8]

- **Happy Environment.** A well-planned time schedule helps to distribute household chores among family members, avoid over-commitments, and maintain a peaceful and happy environment.

- **Personal Growth.** One gets time for knowledge gaining, hobbies, health-care exercises, and self-care. These contribute to the fulfilling of personal life.

- **Stronger family Relationships.** Effective time management allows us more time with family, reducing conflicts arising from late coming and showing neglect towards family members.

Long Commutes

- **Productivity Boost.** By proper planning of time, commuting can be converted into productive activities like listening to audiobooks or planning your day.

- **Reduced Stress.** Proper planning for your commute can minimize the anxiety and frustration often associated with road conditions, traffic jams and weather.

- ◆ **Relax and Recoup**. A long commute can offer a mental break between work and home life. One cold switch off, relax and get set for the day ahead.

Effective Time Management Guidelines. [9]. Some guidelines are briefly given in succeeding paragraphs.

- ◆ **Be Time Conscious.** All successful leaders are time conscious, since they appreciate real value of time. Time is more than money since any delay in delivery can adversely impact one's image in the market/ brand name and customers for getting repeat orders. More on this is covered in Chapter 3.

- ◆ **Realistic Goal Setting.** Every organization and every professional must have his/her well-set goals. It relates to achievable goals both as short terms (2-3 Years) as well as long terms (5 Years or more). Goal should be based on SMART principles. SMART is related to S - Specific, M – Measurable, A - Achievable, R – Realistic and T-Time Bound.

- ◆ **Know one's Job.** It is important to know about one's job requirements and responsibilities. One should also know own organizational structure and team capabilities. One may buy or hire additional resources to meet requirements/expectations of the customers and the organization. More on this is covered in chapter 4.

- ◆ **Know One-self.** It is very important to know own competence and deficiencies/gaps related to achieving one's goals. These gaps should be filled urgently. More on this is covered in chapter 5.

- ◆ **Get Organized and work efficiently.** It is important to use available time efficiently and as per priorities of various tasks. For this, one should be well organized at the workplace, keeping only essential things on the table and rest of the items should be kept away to avoid distraction. Keeping a diary/desk calendar or weekly engagement chart on the wall, helps to keep track of tasks to be done.

♦ **Communicate more effectively.** Be clear and un-ambiguous while communicating or assigning tasks to your team/individual team member. Similarly, be clear while negotiating with customers, vendors and business partners. This will avoid any misunderstanding/misinterpretation and holding short meetings to clarify doubts.

♦ **Better Team Management.[11]** If one is a Team Leader (TL) or Project Manager (PM), beside his/her own commitment, one should deploy own team judiciously and get maximum overall team productivity. Develop good working relationship among team members and trust them.

♦ **Delegate Judiciously. [8]** One should not feel "Know-all" and accumulate more jobs on own table/workbench. Based on the competence and capacity of team members, one should delegate certain parts of the jobs to others .As a leader one must trust them and hold them accountable for the assigned task/responsibility. This will give some free time to the team leader to do more important tasks and also opportunity for others to "Learn by Doing".

♦ **Time Distractors.** One should identify what all people or activities that are taking away his/her valuable time and one must avoid those time destroyers. For instance, some people spend lot of their productive time in social media interaction say on WhatSapp, Twitter (X), Facebook, and LinkedIn or in responding to pop-ups/notifications, which appear on their workstation. More on this is given in chapter 6.

♦ **Time Savers.** It is useful to prepare "To-Do" lists for a day, for a week and for a month and prioritize. One should use emerging technologies to automate operations of certain equipment, appliances and machines both at workplace and at home. More on this is given in chapter 7.

♦ **Time Planning, Monitoring and Control.** What is planned for the execution must be monitored and controlled. For this, appropriate time measuring instruments and tools should be employed. More on this is covered in chapter 11.

♦ **Time for Professional improvement.** One needs to find time and additional resources to learn additional skills and fill the gaps in one's CV. For this, one needs to plan his/her time while at home, while commuting and while doing one's job at the workplace. One should seek approval of the boss to work from home on certain days when one could be attending some skill-building program. Likewise, encourage and support the team members, who are seeking time to learn new skills,

♦ **Time Sharing/Multi-tasking.** In today's global and competitive market, time is a critical resource. One may do time sharing/multi-tasking selectively and get some breather. One must spare time for children, elders and also for friends. More on this is covered in chapter 13.

Summary. Time and opportunities do not wait and many events keep happening all around us. It is up to us to plan our time effectively to up-skill ourselves and our teams. The teams should be deployed judiciously within own country or abroad. Comprehensive planning and effective utilization of time will enhance the productivity and profitability of the organization. Delegate certain parts of the job to team judiciously and hold them responsible. This way one can achieve maximum overall team productivity. Develop good working relationship among team members and trust them.

One needs to split 24 hours into small time blocks and allocate those judiciously to the teams to fulfill their assigned responsibilities. Remember, transparency in dealing with people and being true to one's commitment to the customers, vendors and business partners, enhances one's credibility among them. Therefore, one must evolve an appropriate strategy to balance the time both for doing the job efficiently and fulfill family responsibilities willingly.

02

TIME IS A CRITICAL RESOURCE

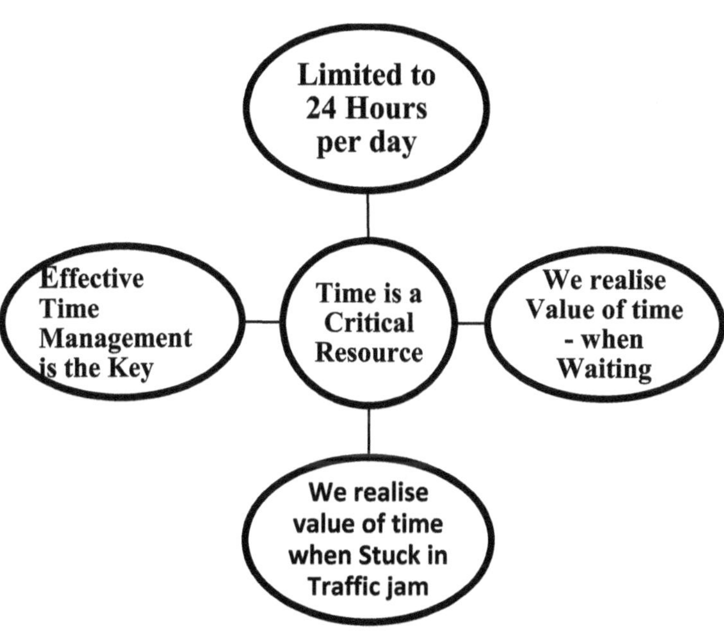

Figure 2.1 Time is a Critical Resource

"Until you value yourself, you will not value your time. Until you value your time, you will not do anything with it."

– M. Scott Peck

Many people often say, "Time is Money". However, Time is more than money, since money can be earned, barrowed and returned but not the time. Time is freely available to everyone but limited to only 24 hours in a day/night. Time continues to move on like flow of river water, which once gone past, cannot return to where one is standing. Likewise, time gone past today will not come back tomorrow.

Every new day brings new hope and new opportunities/challenges. Indeed, time is the most valuable and critical resource for everyone, be it a simple Home-Maker or Motor Mechanic or Student or Doctor or Lab Technician. One could be a Construction Engineer or Production Manager, Transport Driver, Train/Metro-rail Driver, Aircraft Pilot, Publicity and Advertising Manager or a Research Scientist. It is very important for everyone to realize true-value of time. It is still more important that the time available to every professional must be effectively managed by him/her. Effective management of time can lead to greater success in job and happiness at home. On the other hand, miss-management of time can cause health issues, mistrust, a feeling of being overwhelmed and drop in productivity, delays and failures to meet deadlines and friction in the family. Ineffective time management can result in loss of Customers, Vendors and Business Partners and unhappiness at home.

Attributes of Time. [9] The true value of time becomes actually apparent in situations where we are forced to wait in long queues, traffic jams, delayed public transport/flights/trains/boats. These experiences underscore the fact that time, once wasted/lost, cannot be reclaimed. Some important attributes related to time which should be kept in mind while planning time utilization, are briefly given below:

♦ **Time is Irreplaceable.** Time is not static but continuously moving and once a moment of time is gone, we can't get it back.

- **Time is Limited.** Unlike money or materials, time is limited to just 24 hours in a day/night. Out of this, we only get say 8 to 10 hours to do our job, 2-3 hours for household chores and balance is spent in travelling, resting, sleeping etc. Realization of finite nature of time propels us to make the best of every minute.

- **Time is Money.** It is well known that every minute spent productively contributes to the earning for the organization. Time helps us to work and earn to achieve our financial goals and meet responsibilities towards the family.

- **Time is Opportunity.** Time provides us opportunity to take action, make progress and achieve success. However, success does not happen by chance. It requires putting in time and effort to learn required skills, practice those in real life and work with determination towards achieving one's goals. Each moment of time is an opportunity to learn new things and contribute to our growth as well as enhance productivity of the organization.

True Value of Time. Time is one of the most valuable resources for achieving success in our chosen career and leading happy family life. We all know time is limited to say 8-10 hours at workplace and 2-3 hours at home for the family, 1-2 hours in commuting to workplace and 1-2 hour for morning household chores and healthcare. The real value of time is realized while waiting in long queues, waiting for the train/bus, stuck in traffic jam and getting late for the concert, as that will start on-time. While realizing importance of time, most of us wish that we should have got at least two hours extra in a day, to complete our job at our workplace and spending joyful time with our family. Some examples of realizing true value of time are briefly given in succeeding sub paragraphs.

♦ **Long Waiting Queues.** We all know waiting time in a long queue outside a general store, on a bus stand, on a railway station ticket counter or on an airport booking counter is quite annoying.

♦ **Waiting for flight Arrival/Departure.** Long waiting for flights to arrive/depart is very annoying. Sometimes passengers miss their connecting flight for undue delay in the incoming flight. Those airlines, whose flights are often delayed, will lose their customers.

♦ **Waiting in traffic Jam.** While we are commuting to the workplace, there could be traffic jam due to road repair or some road accident. If one has not catered for such contingency and does not have cushion time, one could be very uncomfortable, since time is clicking away and one is getting late for his/her work. In a similar road traffic jam situation, one could be just missing his/her flight, train or appointment with the doctor. In these situations, one realizes value of time and could have planned better.

♦ **Class Room Waiting.** Academic Dean/HOD would have scheduled various classrooms and timings, where the designated teacher shall impart instructions to the students of his/her class. If some student is late, he/she may be marked absent and may be allowed to attend the class. However, if all students are in the class room and seated, as per seating plan but the teacher is late, there will be murmur in the class and students will be upset. This waiting time is very annoying. Likewise, the teacher is required to complete the subject within the allotted time and clear the way for new class and teacher to come in.

If starting and finishing of the class is not on time, it will have ripple effect. Frequently late coming teacher will soon get a memo from his/her HOD/Dean of Academics.

♦ **Reaching Examination Hall.** We all know for any examination, we must reach few minutes before start time, be seated and wait for the invigilator/examiner to distribute the question papers. If we are getting late on our way to the examination centre, we would curse ourselves for not starting early.

♦ **Planning Answering Questions.** While, starting answering the questions in the examination hall, one needs to be time conscious for the length of paper/ number of questions. One must consider weightage of marks and complexity of each question to tackle it first or later. The real value of time is felt when invigilator announces last 5 minutes and we are yet to answer say two questions. We will not have enough time even to revise our other answers. We feel stressed and wish we had 10 more minutes to complete our answers.

♦ **Waiting in OPD Department of a hospital.** If patients are arriving as per their appointment and forming a queue but duty doctor is late, patients will be very upset. In OPD, late arrival of patient is not critical as he/she will get his/her turn little later but doctor coming on time and start his/her work is critical. The patients and doctors both must value the time. Doctors who do not value time, will lose their clients/patients and even lose their jobs.

♦ **Waiting in Justice Court.** If our case for hearing has been scheduled in a particular court room at a particular date and time, we and our attorney plus witnesses if any, must be present near the court room, so that when a call is made, we and our team must be present in front of the judge on time else our case may be single party decision by the judge and we may suffer a big loss.

♦ **Baton Changing in Relay Race.** We have seen 4x4 relay race as how each athlete of four members team runs fast to hand over the baton to the next waiting member on the race track. Any delay by a team member in 2nd or 3rd position, will make it very difficult to make up for the time lost and win the race. All these athletes know the value of every second. The track judges take help of track cameras, in addition to stop watch to decide on photo finish (Split Second).

♦ **Going to Music Concert.** There could be a Music concert or Dance Competition organized in a nearby theatre. The organizers would have publicized the Venue, Date, Time, and names of Artists. People would have bought tickets and anxious to reach the theater and be seated on time to enjoy the event. Imagine if one is stuck in traffic jam and program is just to start. That person is now under stress/tension about reaching late, not getting parking space but the show would start as scheduled. In such situation one appreciates the value of proper planning and reaching the theatre on–time. Another situation could be that audience is seated and waiting for the show to begin but the artists are late or their instruments have not yet reached the theatre. The audience will be restless, and cursing the organizers. The organizers will be under greater stress and trying to locate and hasten arrival of the artists. During this waiting time, playing some trailer of some popular movie may calm down the crowd. This waiting time causes lots of stress and anxiety to the audience and bad name for the organizers.

◆ **Just-In-Time (JIT) Operations.** We all know that to optimize any manufacturing process, smart companies adopt JIT policy for their raw material or semi-finished goods to arrive. Likewise, dispatch of finished and inspected goods must reach the customer on-time. However, any delay in shipping/ delivery will disrupt the manufacturing and delivery chain. In such situation, the production manager feels the pinch of time, stressed and wishes better synchronization of incoming of stores and outgoing finished goods.

◆ **Time Synchronization.** Processing industry could be an Oil Refinery, Food Processing plant, Drink Bottling plant, Fertilizer plant or a Cement plant. These all have sequence of various processes and some processes could be preceding or following. All these have inter-dependent processes where a delay at any stage will have spoiling effect on the following processes. The plant manager and his shift supervisors know the importance of time synchronization and timely correct action by everyone in the chain.

◆ **Project Delivery Deadline.** If one is a delivery manager and running tight on schedule, he/she knows the value of time, since customer may impose penalty clause as given the contract for delayed delivery. When the project in running behind schedule, one will ask the team to rush up and that can cause drop in quality. We all know that a product which is not meeting required quality standards will be rejected by the customer and we have to rework at our own cost, effort and time. Thus every delivery manager is conscious of time. Repeated delays in few projects will tarnish brand name in the market and the organization will lose customers and even business partners.

♦ **Business Alliances.** We all know that every progressive company would like to have alliance with a business partner who has the reputation of delivering on time. These business partners expect us to be on time, be it a video conference or any other interaction. One needs to be time conscious, particularly when dealing with global partners. Global business partners know the true-value of Time and value of Time Zones. They expect similar response from us, else we will lose them. Therefore, realizing true-value of time by all those participating in the business chain is very essential.

♦ **Home Makers.** A home maker who looks after household affairs knows the true value of time. She does multi-tasking, like making breakfast and tiffin for sending children to school on time. She ensures that her children do not miss their school bus and they must carry their books and tiffin. She also helps her working spouse to get ready fast and leave home on time, to reach his workplace on time.

♦ **Response Time.** In technology driven era, speed is the order of the day. We all know that while working on a computer/laptop/tablet or smart phone, we expect very fast response to our query. Any delay of more than two seconds is quite irritating and some of us start bashing the keyboard or twisting our fingers or biting our nails. At this stage, we are looking at the blank screen till computing device responds and we realize the real value of time. Similarly, for on-line answering customer's query, our website must provide fast response time to all on-line searches/queries. Indeed, we all wish that response could be faster. Similarly, if our response is slow to customer requirement he/she will leave our web site and go elsewhere. Thus delayed response can cost us losing customers and goodwill in the market.

Strategies to maximize the Value of Time. [9] Strategies and techniques for effective management of time have been covered in details in chapter 12. Some popular strategies for maximizing value of time are listed below:

♦ **Preparing To-Do lists.** To save time and meet deadlines one must prepare To-Do lists of tasks to be performed in one day, in one week and in one month.

♦ **Prioritization.** From the To-Do lists, identify the most important tasks using Eisenhower Matrix and put focus on those.

♦ **Time Management Techniques.** Use techniques like time blocking, and Pomodoro Technique.

♦ **Minimize Distractions.** Create a focused work environment and eliminate/manage distractions.

♦ **Effective Time Management Tools.** Utilize tools like calendars, task management apps and time tracking software.

♦ **Continuous Learning.** Investing time in learning new skills and knowledge pays rich dividends.

Change with Times. Way back in 1946, Mahatma Gandhi, Father of Indian Nation had said *"Change is the Spice of Life"*. Change with time is natural phenomena and unstoppable. In last 10 years, many things and business practices have changed, where technology has taken quantum jump and it continues to change rapidly. Consequently, many new business practices and working across many time-zones on a 24x7 basis have come in to practice. As such, we too need to change fast, and quickly learn new technologies which are impacting time management.

Summary. By understanding the true value of time and implementing effective time management strategies, we can significantly enhance our productivity, reduce stress, and achieve our goal. It is well known that time is the most critical resource for any organization or an individual professional. Therefore, available time must be managed effectively. One must seriously analyze own competence and that of the team and get rid of time-distractors. It is important to stay focused and gainfully utilize available time to enhance productivity at the workplace and happiness at home.

03

TIME CONSCIOUSNESS

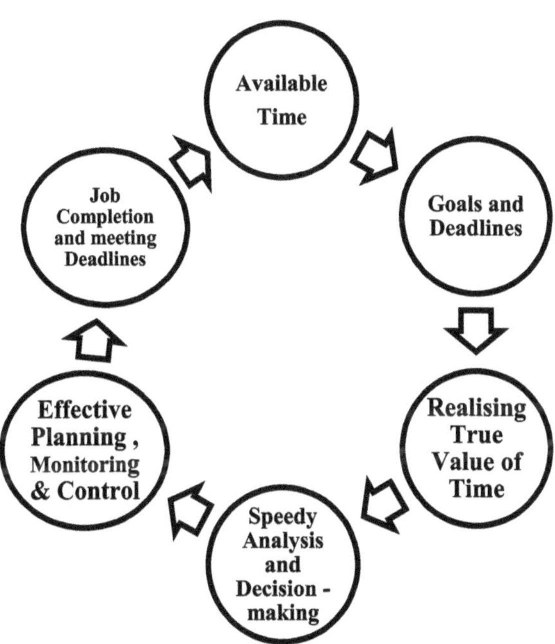

Figure 3.1 Typical cycle of Time Consciousness

Time is the most valuable coin in your life. You and you alone will determine how that coin will be spent. Be careful that you do not let other people spend it for you",´

– John Dryden

It is well known that to appreciate the real value of time and use it effectively, one needs to be time-conscious. Time consciousness is essentially, being proactive and alert to various distractors and emerging opportunities. It helps us to handle distractors tactfully and use available time effectively. Time consciousness helps in timely and more informed decision-making. As such, time consciousness is the foundation upon which all good time management techniques are built. All successful leaders are time-conscious since they know the real value of time. They will not allow even a minute to be wasted. They are proactive, fast thinkers and make information-based decisions. They are highly responsive to any emerging situation and quickly initiate appropriate action to tackle it effectively. They do not waste time in thinking, hoping and waiting. Some advantages related to time consciousness are briefly given below:

- **Helps mitigating Distraction.** Time consciousness helps an individual and his/her team to mitigate distractions and stay focused on the task at hand. This improves the productivity of the organization.

- **Helps improve Discipline.** Time consciousness makes us realize real-value of time. Indeed, it acts as a powerful motivator to stay disciplined, reach and leave workplace on time and work with full energy and determination.

- **Helps to avoid Procrastination.** Procrastination is the biggest time destroyer and is also called *"Pyrolysis through Analysis (PTA)"*. It makes one hesitate to take a decision and time passes away. On the other hand, if one is time conscious, he/she will be aware of deadlines and the time commitments made to various customers and senior management. Hence, he/she will do a quick analysis and start the job with full enthusiasm.

- **Enhances Creativity.** When we are time-conscious, we can allocate specific time blocks for creative thinking, idea generation and achieve excellence.

- **Facilitates goal setting.** Time consciousness helps one to set realistic goals by following the SMART strategy.

- **Facilitates Prioritizing Tasks.** When we are conscious of time, we can easily prepare To-Do lists and prioritize various tasks more effectively.

- **Improved Decision-Making.** Time consciousness allows us to make timely and well-informed decisions. This avoids making impulsive decisions in a hurry which could be rash.

- **Helps in Planning.** It helps one to draw realistic schedules for executions of jobs and meet deadlines. One would know available resources 5 Ms. - Manpower (Workforce), Material, Machinery/ Equipment, Money (Funds) and Method (How to do). One would also know the capacity/capability of his/her team and prepare better time estimates. This will avoid overloading of oneself and the team. It also avoids crisis management.

- **Helps in Monitoring and Control.** Time conscious person will track progress by regular monitoring and initiate in-process control.

- **Facilitates Effective Utilization of Time.** Time consciousness is crucial for making judicious allocation of time-blocks for various tasks.

- **Facilitates Focus.** If one is time conscious, he/she can easily focus his/her energy and utilize available time for achieving one's goals.

- **Increased Productivity.** By being aware of time, we can prioritize tasks, allocate time effectively and quickly start execution of the allotted tasks.

- **Stronger Relationships.** Time-conscious professionals can develop stronger relationships at his/her workplace and spend sufficient time with family.

- **Reduces Stress.** Time consciousness aids effective time management, which can help to reduce stress and anxiety. This helps in keeping good health and leading a more balanced life.

  Developing Time Consciousness. [8] To develop time consciousness, one will require proper strategy and time-measuring tools. Some common techniques to develop time consciousness are briefly given below:

- **Analyze your Time Utilization.** One should keep a record for a few days, as to how he/she actually spends the time. This can be an eye-opener and help one to identify distractors, which are eating up time and reducing productivity.

- **Minimize Distractions.** Create a focused work environment and eliminate all distractions.

- **Realistic Goals.** One should not try to do too many tasks in a day. Instead, one should set achievable goals and allocate enough time and resources for each task. One should set his/her goal clearly by adopting a SMART (Specific, Measurable, Achievable/Attainable, Relevant/Realistic, and Time-bound) strategy.

- **Prioritize Tasks.** Identify important tasks as (MSC), Must (M) do, Should (S) do and Could (C) do and allocate adequate time blocks accordingly.

- **Time Management Techniques.** Utilize time management techniques like Time Blocking, Pomodoro Technique, and Eisenhower Matrix.

- **Delegate judiciously.** One should not feel "Know-all" and invite all jobs on his/her table, as that will make him/her a bottleneck. Instead, give the team members an opportunity to become time-conscious and perform to grow. Delegate various tasks as per the capability and capacity of team members and hold them responsible.

- **Do not answer every Tele Calls.** One must value one's time, which is limited. Therefore, put the mobile phone on vibrate/silence/Aeroplane mode. Ignore and discard calls from unknown numbers. Be selective and call back only when convenient.

- **Put off Notifications and Screen Pop-ups.** One should turn off all notifications coming as popup on his/her laptop/tablet/smartphone. These could be commercial advertisements or spam. If one allows popups on his/her computer screen, these popups will distract and take one away to some other website.

- **Quiet Working Place.** One should find a quiet place to work when one needs to focus on some important task. If one is working in a cabin, close the door and place a notice outside.—*"Don't Disturb"*

- **Regularly Review and Adjust.** Regularly assess your time management strategies and make adjustments as needed.

Summary. Time consciousness is a powerful tool that can significantly enhance our productivity and overall quality of life. Time consciousness helps in appreciating the real importance of time and the necessity to plan and utilize available time more efficiently. If one is time-conscious, one will realize that the true value of time is more than that of money. Consequently, one becomes more effective in managing available time as well as time of his/her team. Indeed, time consciousness helps in achieving higher productivity, better quality of products/services and leading a happy family life.

04

KNOW YOUR JOB

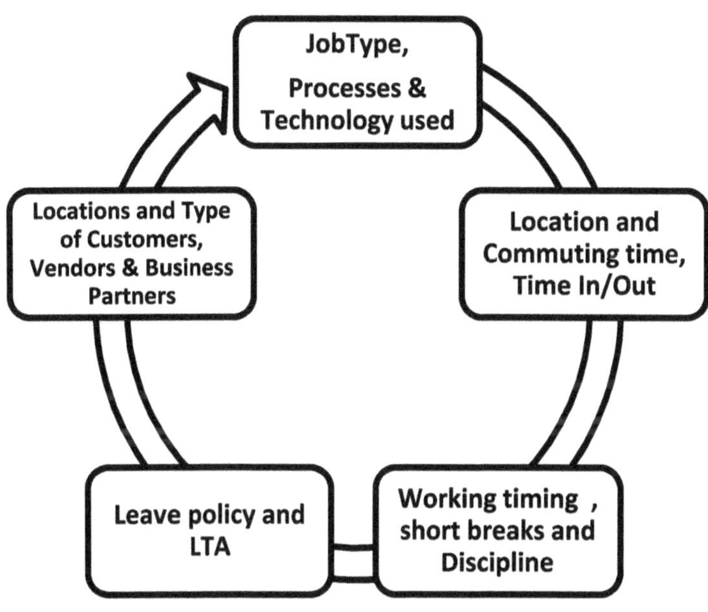

Figure 4.1 Job contents and Responsibilities

"Good to know how much you know but more important is to know how much you don't know and fill those gaps urgently"

– Anonymous

Knowing one's job and fully understanding one's responsibilities are the foundation for effective time management. One could be working in areas like Construction (Roads/bridges, buildings, towns), Road Transport, Railways, Aviation, Process Industries (Fertilizer, Cement, Food Processing or Refinery), Agriculture, Tele-Communications, Education, Healthcare services, IT Enabled Services (IES), Software development company, Sales, Advertisement and Mass communications. It may be any department of the government at the centre /state level. It is the responsibility of everyone to be clear about one's job. To perform efficiently at one's workplace and lead the team from the front, one must be familiar with his/her job, Technology in use, its Business Processes, Standing Operating Procedures (SOPs), Policy on Quality, Ethos, Work Culture, Customers, Vendors and Collaborations/Business Partners.

There could be dispersed teams, deployed within the country and overseas. Issuing of clear instructions on discipline related to dress code, on-time reaching and leaving the workplace and following clear instructions for short break time is important. Likewise, knowledge of rules and regulations regarding Earned Leave, Medical leave, Casual Leave, Annual Leave and LTA helps in planning holidays with the family. Understanding one's job responsibilities is crucial for maintaining a healthy work-life balance. By having a clear understanding of the job responsibilities, one can manage one's time better, reduce stress, and create a better work-life balance.

Importance of knowing own job. [9] A good understanding of one's job/and responsibilities is very important for effective time management. Salient points are briefly given below:

- ◆ **Aids in Prioritizing Tasks.** Knowing one's specific duties and responsibilities helps to prioritize tasks and allocate time judiciously.

♦ **Awareness of Resources.** Being aware of available resources 5 Ms. (Manpower, Material, Machinery (/Equipment,/Tools, Instruments, Technology), Method and Money (Allocated Budget) helps in efficient planning and execution.

♦ **Communication Channels.** Understanding the organizational structure and reporting lines helps in fast decision-making, seeking assistance when needed and reporting progress.

♦ **Culture and Customs.** One needs to be familiar with the culture/customs of the organization as well as those of business partners and overseas teams. This brings harmony and mutual respect.

Benefits of Job Understanding. Good Knowledge of one's job has the following benefits:

♦ **Aids Self Improvement.** Knowing one's job is like having a roadmap for reaching one's destination. A good understanding of one's job helps in identifying areas for self-improvement and the improvement of team members.

♦ **Career Advancement.** If one knows his/her job fully, one can easily identify additional qualifications/skills needed to perform well. Accordingly, one can plan to learn new skills, become more efficient and rise faster in career.

♦ **Popularity.** A good understanding of one's role and show-casing strong time management skills can lead to praise by all and one stays in demand.

♦ **Helps task prioritization.** A clear understanding of one's job responsibilities helps him/her to identify high-priority tasks. This allows for prioritizing the workload and allocating time blocks judiciously.

- **Efficient Resource Allocation.** It helps in the judicious allocation and utilization/reutilization of available resources, which saves in terms of cost, time and effort.

- **Facilitate Resources Planning.** It is part of one's job to know the resources available to him/her. Resources may include team members, time of other experts, technology, equipment, tools/instruments and management support. This knowledge will allow one to plan the resources more effectively.

- **Efficient Time Allocation.** Knowing one's job involves understanding the resources one needs to accomplish one's tasks. If one has clarity of one's job requirement, responsibilities and resources available, one can allocate resources and time judiciously.

- **Facilitate Effective Time Management.** A clear understanding of one's workload allows one to prioritize tasks and effectively manage available time.

- **Facilitate Setting Boundaries between work and home.** When one knows his/her responsibilities at the workplace and at home, it is easier to set boundaries between work and personal life. This helps in preventing burnout at the workplace and conflicts at home.

- **Helps Effective Communication.** Understanding one's role enables to communicate effectively with his/her employer, customers, vendors, team members, peers and business partners. In turn, it boosts productivity and better growth of the organization.

- **Enduring Collaborations.** Knowing the roles and capabilities of team members of local and distant teams facilitates setting realistic deadlines.

Likewise, knowing the capabilities and resources of business partners helps in establishing an enduring collaboration.

◆ **Quality Policy.** Knowing one's job helps in adhering to quality standards of the organization. This ensures that work is done on **"First Time Right"** basis. It avoids rework and ensures meeting deadlines without time/cost over-runs.

◆ **Reduces Stress.** A clear understanding of expectations of seniors reduces anxiety and helps in stress-free working. One could be proactive and meet those expectations and prevent unnecessary stress and delays.

◆ **Knowing Work Culture.** Understanding of one's job involves knowing about organization's work culture, priorities, ethos and values. This in turn, helps to align one's tasks with the overall goals of the organization.

Guidelines for better understanding of job. On joining an organization, the HR department will provide various documents related to the assigned job, policies and ethos of the organization. There will be lot to learn from on-the-job as you progress in your carrier. Some basic guidelines are briefly given below:

◆ **Observe and Learn.** Be alert and pay attention to how experienced colleagues handle similar tasks. This is the fastest and well proven way of learning.

◆ **Seeking Clarification.** One should not hesitate to ask his/her superior or colleagues or even juniors for clarification of doubts. This will ensure right action on right time.

◆ **Seek Feedback.** Regularly seek feedback from the superior to identify areas for improvement.

- **Stay Updated.** It is important to stay updated about any changes in work policies, procedures, organizational structure and even government policies as related to the type of job. One should periodically review the documents related to job description and policies of the organization, since these do change with time.

Summary. A clear understanding of one's job and the expectations of the organization can help one to create a focused work environment and minimizing distractions. Adherence to the organizational policies and norms ensures smooth operations and avoids delays/wrong actions. By investing time in understanding one's job, one can significantly enhance one's time management skills and overall productivity. If one clearly knows his/her job contents, responsibilities and resources, one can be proactive and plan to allocate time blocks for various tasks judiciously. Indeed, good knowledge of the job helps in effective time management and maintaining work-life balance. Regularly reflecting on one's work performance and seeking feedback can help to identify areas for improvement. A person having full knowledge of his/her job is well respected by team members, seniors and business partners.

05

KNOW YOURSELF

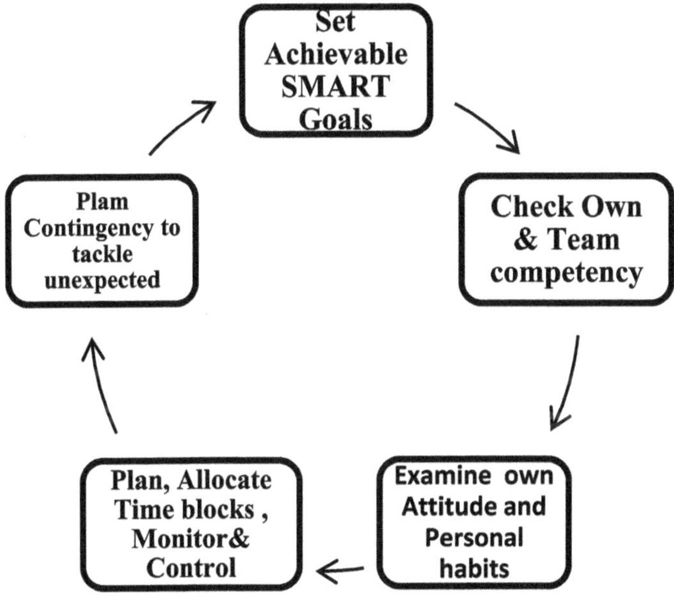

Figure 5.1 Self-Audit using SWOT Analysis

"Focusing your life solely on making a quick buck shows a poverty of ambition. It asks too little of yourself. And it will leave you unfulfilled". Barak Obama,

– USA President.

For effective time management, one should know oneself in terms of personal habits, capability and deficiencies and plan to quickly fill up the gaps. It is equally important to know the capability of one's team and provide them opportunities to equip themselves with new skills. It is good to know how much one knows but more important is to know how much one does not know and from where/whom to know what one does not know. Once he/she knows from where to know, he/she should not delay and just go for it. This action will make one knowledgeable and in demand.

We all have different family backgrounds, education type/level, financial status, personality, attitude, aptitude and professional competency. Some of us are well organized and highly efficient in our jobs, while others are less organized and casual about time. Those who are less organized obviously will spend their time in wasteful activities like searching for books/files/notes or tools. Such people easily get distracted by others and lose their focus on completing the job at hand. In order to plan and utilize available time gainfully, grow in one career and flourish in life, one should be time conscious and do self-audit regularly, using the SWOT analysis technique. This is related to the type and structure of the organization, nature of the job, work environment at the workplace and type/size of family.

Own Capability Assessment. The following are the points to be checked and assessed:

- ◆ **Know your Dream.** Everyone should have a dream in life. To make one's dream come true, one needs to have required qualification and competency.

- ◆ **Know your Passion.** Everyone should have passion. This relates to one's inner fire which will propel one towards the "Path of excellence".

- ◆ **Know your Goals.** It is important for every individual to have his/her goals both short-term and long-term. One needs to check on the following:

- ◆ Does one has a dream and how will he/she fulfill that?

- ◆ What are one's short-term (1-3 Years) goals?

- ◆ What are one's long-term (5-7 years) goals?

- ◆ What is one's life-time goal?

- ◆ What kind of position one wishes to be, in 5 years and 10 years?

◆ **Know own Learning Style.** One should know his/her learning style and undertake the best learning approach which suits him/her for learning new skills.

◆ **Know Personal Habits.** One needs to review personal habits of reaching and leaving the workplace on time, time spent on household chores and the time spent on getting ready for going to the workplace.

◆ **Know your Strengths and Weaknesses.** One should identify one's areas of expertise and areas where one may need improvement. SWOT analysis will help in this regard.

◆ **Know your Time Utilization.** Everyone should be time-conscious. It is very important to know how one is spending one's time, both at the workplace and at home. It is necessary to know what is eating up one's available time, both at the workplace and at home.

◆ **Know your time for improvement.** One needs to find time to go for learning new knowledge/skills to stay in demand. Up-to-date knowledge is necessary for having a leading role in the organization.

◆ **Know your Job Responsibilities.** To do a job efficiently, one must fully know one's job and responsibilities. One also needs to know what his/her seniors expect out of him/her. One should also know what to do, when to do and how to do or how to get it done.

- **Know your Competency.** One needs to know own competency to achieve one's goals and if there is a deficiency, that must be made up soonest. Therefore, one should periodically, carry out self-analysis/audit, by using the SWOT (Strength, Weakness, Opportunities and Threat) technique. It helps to learn new skills and improves one's competency. Likewise, it is very useful to know the competency of the team members and support them to learn newer skills.

- **Know your Boss/Reporting Line.** [5] One needs to know one's responsibility and chain of reporting. As a principle of professional integrity, one should not bypass one's immediate superior (Boss). One must take instructions from one's boss and faithfully report to him/her.

- **Know Rules and Regulations.** [16] One should know rules and regulations related to own organization, controlling agencies, center/state government, Ignorance of rules is no excuse.

- **Know how well you are organized**. Everyone should be well organized in the workplace. Keep your work table clear of unwanted files/papers or other items which could restrict one's movement or cause distraction. Maintaining a Personal Diary/, Bar-Chart and Engagement Calendar on the wall or in one's laptop/tablet/smartphone can help in keeping track of important events.

- **Know Team Managing.** One needs to check how one is managing his/her team. One may be very efficient individually for some type of job but it is more important to work efficiently as a team member. One should maintain good relationship among team members.

- **Know your delegation strategy.** It is important to check the effectiveness of one's strategy for delegating. One should delegate jobs as per the competency of individuals/teams. One should not take on the extra load with the ego of "Know-all". Instead, one must trust others, give them an opportunity to perform and hold them responsible.

- **Know the reuse of existing Resources.** [14] Discourage people from *"re-inventing the wheel"* for the sake of their ego. Instead of starting from scratch, they should locate already developed modules/sub-assemblies by others and use/modify those to save time.

- **Know your Resources.** One should be fully aware of resources (5Ms) available to him/her in terms of Manpower (Personnel), Material, Machinery (Hardware/software), Money (allocated funds) and Method (Know-How). This will help to avoid any time and cost overruns.

- **Know your Communication skills.** One should know the effectiveness of one's communication skills and improve those as needed. The instructions issued verbally or in writing should be clear with no chance of misunderstanding/misinterpretation by those who are to implement various tasks.

- **Know the effectiveness of Monitoring and Control.** [11] Everyone should regularly monitor and control the progress of various jobs/tasks. While good planning, scheduling of tasks and issuing of clear instructions are very important, regular monitoring and control are equally important for keeping a project on track.

- **Knowledge of Time Distractors.** One should identify what are the time distractors, which are eating up one's time and disturb one's focus. One should find ways and means to avoid/manage time distractors and save time. It is important to check if one is effectively managing the impact of distractors.

- **Know your Self-Discipline Standards.** Everyone should sincerely maintain daily time-in and time-out. One should follow time limits for scheduled breaks. One needs to check if one attends all scheduled meetings and participates actively. A good leader has good self-discipline to inspire others around him/her. One must follow what one preaches.

- **Know your Habits and Etiquette.** One should know what kind of person he/she is. It is related to one's character, attitude, nature/personal habits, behaviour, maturity and integrity.

- **Know your Relationships**. One should have cordial relations with all. It relates to one's relationship with juniors, colleagues and seniors. Good relationship builds mutual respect and trust, which helps one to draw synergy.

Summary. In today's world of fast-advancing AI, ML, Robotics, Drones and other technologies, one cannot stay happy with a one-time qualification and stick on to a job till one retires. One needs continuous learning and up-skilling to stay in demand; otherwise one may lose one's job. There is a nice quote related to self-improvement.

"Build yourself above yourself",

– By Samuel Smiles

We all want success in our jobs and also live a happy family life. For this, we need to organize our work-table better, plan our available time intelligently and work very efficiently, with full focus on the job at hand. One needs to set timelines by which he/she will add the required skills and be well-equipped for the higher job/new job. One should discuss one's plan for self-improvement with one's mentors and inspiring friends. They are well-wisher and will give him/her correct advice. A comprehensive understanding of oneself and one's team is indeed crucial for effective time management.

06

TIME DISTRACTORS

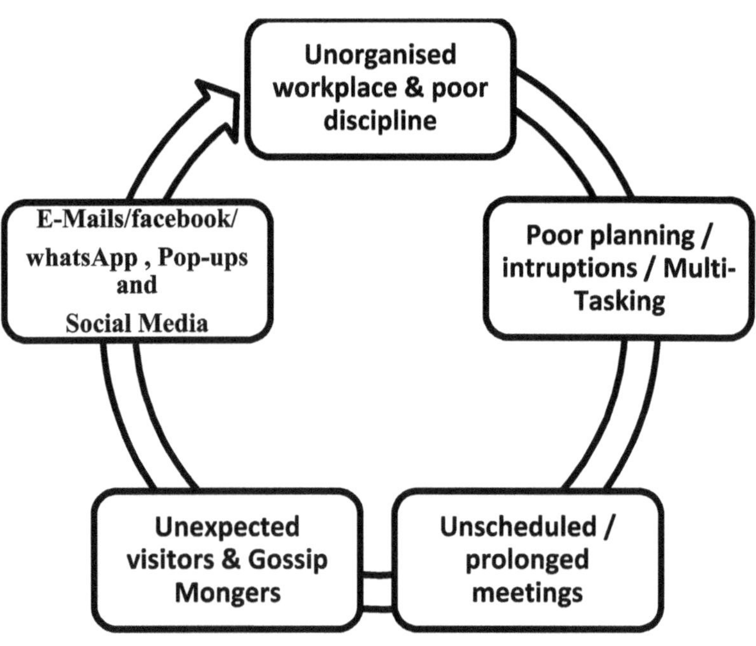

Figure 6.1 Time Distractors/Destroyers

"The world is full of noise and distractions, if you can stay focused on what really matters, you can achieve anything"

– Ton Bilyeu

Time destructors are also known as time destroyers, since these disturb one's focus/concentration and one puts in-progress task on hold and attend to an unexpected/ unimportant new task/job. If the new job is a very small task and it is important, it may be right to take it up this small task and quickly finish it and resume one's main job, which one has just put on hold. One should realize that distractions will reduce one's productivity, since one would be spending time and energy doing unwanted/unscheduled/unimportant tasks. These disruptions will jeopardize one's timeline set for the main job/project. These distractors can be internal or external, and these can come at any time and in many forms. If one has not learnt the art of firmly handling these distractors by saying "NO", one will often get overloaded and he/she and the team will remain stressed out. If one accepts every job without considering load of current projects/jobs, he/she and the team will feel overloaded and become a cause for delays in various important tasks. Consequently, one will resort to crisis management and try to cope by rushing up without worrying about the quality standards. In the long run, it will adversely affect the brand name of the organization in the market and also with business alliances.

Impact of Distractors. Distractors/time destroyers could be of different type as per one's job/position in the workplace and nature of the organization, in which one is working. People could be working in Technology area, Construction of Roads , Bridges, Railway tracks, Buildings or Metros, Mining & Exploration , Chemicals and Oil, Healthcare, Agriculture, Education, Manufacturing, Transport, Design and Architecture, Banking , Publicity and Advertising, Research and Development (R&D) and Government Departments. Different distractors will impact differently on people working in different fields and levels.

Distractors Types and Remedies. If one is working in any organization small/medium/large, one is inter dependent on working of others in the team. Therefore, one has to deal with various distractors as per ethos/work culture of the organization and its rules and regulations. However, If one is working from home as one/two persons ownership of a small business (small entrepreneur), the distractors are local to a limited work environment and one has to deal as per one's personal capacity to work. Some common distractors which one should guard against are briefly given in succeeding sub-paragraphs. Some remedies have also been suggested for dealing with various distractors.

- ◆ **Human Interruptions.** Some colleague may leisurely walk up to one's work desk, just for chatting or persuade him/her for accompanying to the coffee shop/cafeteria. Such colleagues may be having an unscheduled break or just to relax and not concerned about other's work. Be firm to politely decline such unnecessary interruptions. For this, one should learn the art of saying "NO" politely but firmly.

- ◆ **Unscheduled Visitors** (Intruders). These are the intruders which could be a vendor or a customer. Be firm to ask them to wait in the visitor's room or meet some other person or simply decline to meet such intruders.

- ◆ **Physical discomfort.** Feeling hungry, tired, or uncomfortable in the workspace can make it difficult to concentrate on the job. It is the responsibility of HR/Senior Management to provide comfortable seats and workbenches, proper air-conditioning, create good relaxing environment by having a gym, walking park, lawns and fountains , self-help coffee points, food point/canteen/cafeteria like facilities.

- ◆ **Disturbing Noisy Environment.** There could be noise coming from nearby machine or small group of people loudly discussing some topic/issue. This can disturb one's focus/concentration. Of course, such interruptions apply only to office/chair-bound jobs and not to the fields like Agriculture, Transportation, Construction work (Roads, Bridges, Railways Tracks or Shopping Malls/Housing complexes, Process Control Plants (Cement, Fertilizer, Food/Milk, Chemical and Oil industry) or Marketing/Sales.

♦ **Screen Pop ups and Notifications.** Social media advertisements/business promotion notifications from unknown numbers may just pop up on one's Desktop/Laptop/Tablet/Smart phone. These notifications can show up along one's emails, WhatsApp or Twitter (X) messages. Therefore, one must turn off notifications/pop-ups on one's smart phone/tablet and computer screen. Popping up notifications will distract and suggest attending to those. If one attends to such pop ups, one will lose one's focus and precious time.

♦ **Browsing unrelated websites.** Most of the screen pop up are cleverly designed to take the person away to other websites. One may be tempted to put on hold one's job-in-hand and go for browsing unrelated websites. Any browsing on unrelated websites is major time destroyer and need to be controlled. There should be strict warning in the work policy/ work culture and work-ethos of the organization that while doing a job, there will not be any browsing on unofficial websites. Defaulters should be warned once or twice and thereafter strict disciplinary action should be taken to curb such unlawful/wasteful activities.

♦ **Procrastination.** Procrastination/Vacillating or Hesitating is a state of indecisiveness, which happens when a complex/difficult task is repeatedly put on hold. This situation is also called *"Pyrolysis through*

Analysis (PTA)". Such people keep thinking/ analyzing, hesitating and postponing decision, till the last minute and then work under stress in a hasty way, resulting in more errors and rework. Putting off important/complex task until the last minute can lead to stress and confusion. Hence, we should follow simple management principle- "First Thing First" and carryout each job efficiently. In fact, difficult or more complex task should be broken down into simpler and smaller modules, which are easy to execute, monitor and control.

◆ **Lack of Planning.** Not having prepared To-Do lists and not prioritizing of tasks will lead to poor planning and poor allocation of Time Blocks. This can lead to waste of time and confusion about priorities. To offset this confusion, one need to prepare To-Do lists which should be for a day, for a week and for a month. Examine To-Do lists carefully and prioritize various tasks, as urgent, important and unimportant and allocate adequate blocks of time for various tasks.

◆ **Multi-Tasking.** It is common belief that multi-tasking is based on time sharing and it can save some time and improve productivity. Some people feel themselves "know-all" and over confident of their working capacity/capability. They often undertake multi-tasking, thinking they can concurrently handle multiple jobs and save time. This is not always true, since multi-tasking leads to overload and consequently drop in quality/efficiency. It is better to handle "first-thing-first" or follow "First in First out (FIFO)" principle and stay focused to get better results. This will ensure on-time delivery of pre-scheduled tasks and not keeping many tasks in a state of Work-in-Progress (WIP).

- **Perfectionism.** Some professionals are perfectionists and want to achieve 100% perfection in the product before delivering to the customer, even it overshoots timeline. However, as a good business practice, it is always better to be 90% or even 80% right but operational and deliver the product/project on time, with the promise that rest will be delivered by a date.

- **Poor Communication. [12]** If communication by the project manager/team leader is not clear, there is risk of misunderstanding resulting in mismatch with Customer Requirement (CR). Consequently, it will result in reworking due to rejection in quality by the inspection team. Poor communication will result in too many meetings to clarify doubts/misunderstanding and reschedule timeline. This will cause overall delay in delivery of the project and dissatisfaction of the customer.

- **Prolonged Meetings.** While business meetings are important to review status of a job/project, but poorly planned and informally conducted meetings can stretch beyond the scheduled time. There can be also unscheduled meeting called by the seniors. All these disrupt the workflow and eat up valuable time. As a remedy, agenda for the meeting, time and place should be pre-planned by the seniors and circulated beforehand among all participants. The person conducting the meeting should insist that all participants must be on-time, participate actively and stick to the framework of the circulated agenda. Meeting should be concluded on time so that participants can leave in time to get back to their work places.

- **Unrealistic Goals.** Setting unrealistic goals/deadlines or trying to do too much, with too little resources in a short period can lead to demoralization for the team. Project managers/Team leaders who tend to set unrealistic goals, their teams often fail to deliver on time. Consequently, there will be drop in productivity. Therefore goals should be based on the SMART strategy.

♦ **Unwanted/Untimely Mobile Phone calls.** There could be someone across time-zones, calling on cellphone, just to chat and waste one's time. Such a person is irresponsible, since he/she has not considered others working time. One must be firm to say "call you later" and cut off the call. It is important that while at workplace, one should put one's phone on Airplane mode/Silent mode. One should also tell family members/friends not to call during working hours until there is some emergency.

♦ **Staying longer than Scheduled Breaks.** There are people who are not time conscious and after the scheduled break, they just hang around in the cafeteria, Gym or meditation centre. As a team leader/manager, set clear boundaries for break durations. One may give his/her team lunch break of say 30 minutes, After those 30 minutes, everybody must be back on respective worktable.

Summary. Remember, effective time management is about being aware of how one spends one's time and taking steps to minimize distractions. Therefore, one must plan one's day by creating To-Do lists and schedule blocks of time for specific tasks. By identifying time destroyers, one can develop suitable strategies to mitigate their impact. Be firm to tactfully decline unnecessary interruptions and also decline to entertain unscheduled visitors. One should not accept additional jobs, if one is already fully occupied. For this one should learn the art of saying "NO" politely but firmly.

Based on one's type of job, status/responsibilities in the organization, one needs to evolve appropriate strategies to combat time distractors. By judicious control on one's working environment, one can mitigate impact of time distractors and achieve greater productivity. Effective time management at the workplace will also help in having enough time with the family to enjoy.

07

TIME SAVERS

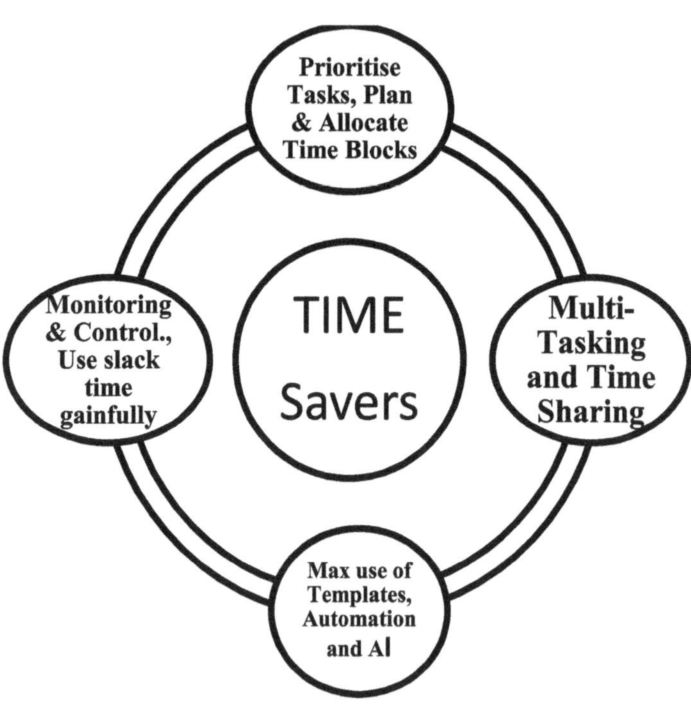

Figure 7.1 Typical Time Saving Environment

"The bad news is time flies. The good news is you're the pilot".

– Michael Altshuler.

Time is very valuable resource for any organization and for every individual, who may be working at any level and in any field. However, maximum time available to any one is only 24 hours, which includes day and night. Therefore, it is essential to save time and utilize it intelligently to ensure maximum productivity at the workplace and peace at home. For this, one must carefully plan own workload and that of his/her team, prioritize various tasks, schedule those tasks intelligently and allocate adequate time blocks. As a team leader or project manager one must plan to save time using various technologies, time measuring tools/instruments and strategies like time-sharing/multi-tasking, delegating, out-sourcing and seeking outside help when needed. This will ensure that all tasks are properly executed to meet deadlines and required quality standards. Time saving is to be done at all times and by all.

Time saving at Home. [9] In a family, there are number of household chores where one is required to do his/her share. These tasks consume time and therefore need to be handled properly. Some of the strategies are briefly given in succeeding sub-paragraphs, while more details are covered in chapter 15.

- ◆ **Grouping similar tasks.** Going to a grocery shop, vegetable/fruit shop, medical store, milk booth and meat shop are daily routine tasks. Some of these tasks can be grouped and carried out in a single visit.

- ◆ **Dust Control for cleanliness.** House cleaning time can be reduced, if we prevent dust coming in from outside. It is well said -*"Prevention is better than Cure"*. Most of the dirt comes in the house through our dirty/dusty shoes or street side open windows. One should prevent such dirt simply by placing a foot-mat at the entrance of the house. One can even take one's shoes off at the entrance door and put in the shoe rack, kept at the entrance. This should also be followed by all family members and the visitors.

Dust can also come through open windows or when there is a dust storm. Therefore keep street side windows closed and even use rubber lining below the doors to stop wind blowing in dust. By taking such simple measures, one requires lesser time for house cleaning.

♦ **Floor cleaning process**. Despite dust control measures, there will be still some dust which needs daily cleaning. To save time, one should streamline floor cleaning process. For this, one should fill a bucket with everything that one needs for cleaning, like cleaning spray, a sponge, a squeegee, a scrub brush and cloth towels. After cleaning a room, use fan to dry up wet floor to avoid anyone slipping and falling down. Of late, many families are using robot for floor cleaning.

♦ **Clean Daily**. One can save time for cleaning by doing a little cleaning every day, instead of piling up for the next day. Importance of daily cleaning should be understood and followed by all family members. A little effort by each family member saves a lot of time and effort of the house keeper.

♦ **Clear out the Clutter**. When house is cluttered with all sorts of items like old shoes, old books, old broken toys and gardening tools, lying all over, one will waste valuable time in locating things, which one needs urgently. One would be shuffling through unnecessary items from room to room. Therefore, we should keep things in proper rack/stand at their proper place and put waste in the dustbin/scrap container.

♦ **Layout of Efficient Kitchen**. One can save time in the kitchen by keeping various utensils and appliances at the right places for handy to use. One should keep required utensils, frying pans, mixers, juicers and containers next to the cooking stove. Likewise, one should keep everything needed to make coffee like coffee maker, coffee beans, coffee mugs, sugar cubes and so on, in the same area. Similarly, keep knives, chopper and cutting board near each other. By just applying common sense (***though not so common***), one can have an efficient kitchen.

♦ **Efficient Cooking Methods**. One can save lots of time by learning the proper way to chop and fry vegetables. Likewise, one may add baking soda or vinegar to water, when boiling eggs for easier shell removal. Multi-tasking like boiling of eggs, making of tea, warming breakfast in the microwave oven are quite common.

♦ **Keep everything in its Right place.** Good old saying is ever true- "***A place for everything and everything in its place***". Therefore, one should keep shoes, socks, hat, walking stick, office bag, office keys, and office-entry tag at their appropriate places. This will avoid losing time in searching for items, while one could be in hurry to leave for the workplace.

♦ **Eat healthy foods and moderately.** Eating healthy foods will give the energy one needs to be productive throughout the day. It is equally important to eat less, particularly, at night. Remember good old saying "***one should eat to live and not live to eat***".

♦ **Sleep On Time**. One should have a set time, say between 8 PM to 10 PM to sleep each night and stick to it. If one goes to sleep late, say later than 11 PM, one will feel tired and lazy, when one gets up in the morning.

♦ **Wake up Earlier**. Good old saying is a useful tip "***Early to bed early to rise makes a person healthy wealthy and wise***". Therefore, sleeping early and waking up early gives extra time in the morning for doing various household chores.

♦ **Get active fast.** If one feels sleepy or drowsy, when one wakes up, one can't get ready fast. Therefore as soon one wakes up, he/she should get up from the bed, walk up to the windows and open the curtains to get some sunlight and fresh air. One should drink a glass of warm water, which will help the metabolism. One may prepare and have tea/coffee as per his/her taste.

♦ **Speed up getting ready.** One must speed up one's time for tooth brushing, shaving, taking shower, wearing dress and doing prayer.

♦ **Restrict TV- watching time.** By limiting TV watching time to say 2 hours a day, one can get some free time, which one can use for more important tasks. One could also record favorite TV shows and watch those later at a convenient time.

♦ **Exercise regularly.** One should regularly exercise. It is the right way to reduce stress, improve one's metabolism and concentration. Therefore, one should do 30 to 40 minutes of physical exercise/Yoga every day.

♦ **Use technology based household Appliances.** Use of technology based appliances can save lots of time. One could be using automatic Washing Machine, Drying Machine, Dish Washer, Microwave Oven and Hot plate/Grill with timer, Food Cooker and Air-conditioner with timer.

♦ **Using To Do -List as a timer.** Checking time as one is getting ready in the morning is a right way to make sure that one is ready on time. One can even use recorded songs or/news on TV as a timer. Some simple examples are listed below:

- Brush teeth and hair during the first song.

- Make breakfast and some coffee during the second song.

- Eat your breakfast and browse through the newspaper, during the third and fourth song.

- Take shower during the fifth song.

- Get dressed during the sixth song.

- Pick up office bag, say bye to the family members and take off for the workplace.

- **Have Nutritious Breakfast.** Good food is the fuel for the human body engine. Balanced diet should be taken at the appropriate time so that one stays healthy and perform efficiently. Therefore, skipping one's breakfast in order to save time is not a good idea. However, one can save time by preparing a quick breakfast like having yogurt, fresh fruit and an egg sandwich, which one can eat quickly and even eat while commuting.

- **Make tonight next day's Lunch Tiffin.** When one is cooking dinner, one can also cook next day's lunch, put in a plastic container and keep it in the fridge. This will save time in the morning.

- **Night before start collecting things.** One should, write his/her To-Do list night before. Collect wallet, laptop, cell phone, office keys, car/motorcycle key and anything else one may need and pack one's bag. Keep the bag next to the door. This will avoid any flap in the morning.

- **Do not go online in the morning.** Resist the temptation to check email or go on social media in the morning, since this will delay one's departure for the workplace.

♦ **Fix strict time to leave the house**. The time one takes to get ready each morning will increase, until one informs to all family members about one's a firm time to leave the house. One must leave on time and every time. Any delay will impact one's reaching the bus/taxi stand or office vehicle pick up spot.

Time Saving at the Workplace. [9]

♦ **Preparing To-Do lists**. One should prepare To-Do list and prioritize the listed tasks for each day. This will ensure that the most important things get done first each day, instead of wasting time on less important things.

♦ **Prioritizing To-Do tasks**. It is most important to plan your workload of a project or a big job into easily manageable tasks and allocate inter task priorities. One should use tools like Eisenhower Towers to prioritize tasks. One may follow simple principle of MSC – Must (M) do, Should (S) do and Could (C) do. Make a table of tasks as Must Do, Should Do and Could do on following considerations:

♦ **Must Do.** These are the critical tasks, as these are due today itself. These tasks could be 1 to 2 in number and of priority 1. These tasks are critical and must be done right now.

♦ **Should Do.** These are challenging and important tasks. These tasks could be 3 to 4 in number and of priority 2. These tasks are important and should be completed within working hours of the day. Old saying is ever true – *"Don't put off till tomorrow what you can do today"*.

♦ **Could Do.** These tasks are not urgent and can be done later. These are also called "over- the- horizon" list.

These tasks could be 5 to 6 in numbers and of priority 3. Time permitting these could also be carried out else these will move to next day schedule and may get new higher priority say priority 2.

- **Focus on priority tasks.** It is important to focus on important tasks and deploy available resources and energy judiciously.

- **Try to beat the clock.** One should set a clear deadline for everything that one needs to get done. One should do his/her best to meet those deadlines.

- **Delegate tasks.** Even if one knows many things, one should not feel "Know all" and overload one's tray with pending work files. One should not be afraid to delegate tasks to others even if one has the capacity to do. This will allow some time to focus on more important tasks and others will gain confidence in doing assigned task.

- **Ask for help.** If one is feeling overwhelmed, he/she should not be shy to ask for help from colleagues, friends, or family members.

- **Take short breaks.** Taking short breaks helps in overall time saving. During short breaks, one is saving time since one will be recouping, reducing stress, and preventing burnout.

- **Stay Focused.** One should decide what is very important, set a timer say for 45 minutes and focus all attention/energy to complete that task.

- **Outsource.** One should focus on what he/she is good at. Stop feeling "know-all" and trying to do everything, just for ego sake. Instead, identify own strengths and leave the rest to other people. Start outsourcing to reliable vendors/sub-contractors.

- **Dealing with personal emails.** Email can be a big time killer. One will be saving lots of time by creating a system for dealing with email quickly and efficiently. Some guidelines are given below:

  - Check email only twice a day.

  - Limit email sessions to 15 minutes.

  - Decide right away what to do with important emails and delete the rest. .Keeping all incoming emails in the inbox indefinitely will slow down opening and navigating the web page. If inbox is full, some important emails will not be accepted by the system.

- **Improve typing skills.** Some people type just with one finger and that is very slow typing. One must do some typing course and learn to type with both hands, using multiple fingers, .By improving one's typing skills, and by learning keyboard shortcuts, one could save a lot of time.

- **Improve Writing Speed.** One can use standard abbreviations and quickly make hand written short notes, during various meetings/conferences. Later on, one can expand those short notes for proper record.

- **Improve Reading Speed.** Do not read left to right, line by line and word by word. Instead, learn rapid reading skills of reading faster without skipping the essentials. One should keep focus in the center of the page and read downward Depending upon document to be read as print or on computer screen, one can adjust reading speed. Indeed, one can save time by rapid reading.

- **Time Sharing and Multi-Tasking.** If one has several small, unrelated tasks that do not require deep focus, multi-tasking might be efficient. For example, one could answer emails while waiting for a download to finish. The terms "time sharing" and "multi-tasking" are often used interchangeably. Time sharing term is commonly used for Operating System (OS) of a computer, where, OS has the ability to share its processing time among multiple users or tasks simultaneously. Each user or task gets a small slice of the CPU's time in quick succession and smaller job gets completed first, while longer job takes more time slices to get completed. Likewise, we as human being can also do more than one task simultaneously and save some time. More on this is covered in Chapter 13.

♦ **Detailed Planning.** To properly utilize available time and meet various time-lines, one must prepare a sound plan. What cannot be planned need not be undertaken for execution. If it is difficult to plan, break it down the big task into small sub-tasks and allocate time for each task judiciously. To manage time effectively, we need to organize our workplace and plan our work load as per available capacity and resources. Some considerations are given below:

♦ **Time blocking.** Schedule specific blocks of time for each task in the To-Do list. This will help one to stay focused and avoid procrastination,

♦ **Monitoring and Control**. What is planned must be regularly measured, in terms of time spent and the progress is made. This will help monitoring, and control and initiate timely action to maintain overall time-line and meet project deadlines. To maintain time-line, we need to carryout in-process control by critically monitoring time elapsed and progress made. Some tools for monitoring project schedule are briefly given below:

- **Gnat chart/Bar chart**. Maintain a Bar chart showing time allocation and status of various tasks. Use various colours to depict progress of tasks and time elapsed.

- **Review Priority**. Priority 1 tasks are frequently reviewed say, 1 to 2 hours interval. Priority 2 tasks may be reviewed once a day and Priority 3 tasks may be reviewed say once a week.

- **Work Calendar**. Do maintain work calendar which could be a work chart hung on the wall in front of the work table/desk. It could be on the laptop/Tablet/Mob Phone or a table/desk Diary.

- **Maximize use of Technology.** Increase automation of various functions at the workplace.

- **Use AI tools**. It includes Chat GPT, Google's Gemini or Microsoft' Copilot to help in providing collated information, on the required subject, which one may modify to fit into own requirement.

- **Use efficient text editors.** Use editor like MS word of Microsoft along with tools like Grammarly for editing, grammar and plagiarism check.

- **Use Templates**. Prepare and use templates to speed up data input

- **Controlling emails.** One can save sometime by controlling emails, WhatsApp and social media messaging.

- **Auto Reply**. One may use auto reply for emails, while one is away from workplace or whenever needed.

- **Control/block notifications**. One can save some time by exercising control/block notifications and pop-ups on his/her workstation/smart phone/tablet.

- **Learn when to Say NO.** If one does not have the time or capacity to take on new jobs, it is good to tactfully but firmly say NO. Accepting unscheduled jobs will overload both the team leader and his/her team. This will cause undue pressure and stress. It is unwise to accept additional load for cheap popularity, since that will adversely affect overall productivity and deadlines of already scheduled tasks.

Time-Saving during Long Commute. Long commuting hours can be a serious drain on one's time and energy. This could cause stress/strain on human body. By incorporating suitable strategy, one can make one's long commuting hours into productive and enjoyable experience. Here are some guidelines to make good use of commuting hours:

- **On-Line Learning.** While sitting in a taxi/chartered bus, metro rail or a boat, one could easily use his/her smart phone to browse and read some on-line books/articles as given below :

  - Have good quality and comfortable headphones to enjoy better listening of e-books, e-magazines/e-articles.

  - Listen to podcasts or audiobooks and enjoy some engaging stories. However, one must ensure that it does disturb co-passengers.

  - Network by connecting with mentors, colleagues or industry professionals through phone calls or virtual meetings.

- **Comfort and Convenience**

  - Carpooling and sharing the ride with others will reduce traffic congestion.

  - Carry snacks and drinks in the bag to stay hydrated and energized during long journey.

- ◆ Organize personal belongings and keep essential items within easy reach.

- ◆ If driving own vehicle, plan suitable route and avoid peak hours.

◆ **Mental and Physical Exercises.**

- ◆ **Deep Breathing.** Do deep breathing exercises and neck exercises. This will reduce stress and improve focus.

- ◆ **Light Exercises.** Use the commute time as a mini work-out session and do light exercises, while sitting in the seat. However, doing exercise should be without inconvenience to co-passengers.

- ◆ **Meditate.** Practice mindfulness exercises to improve mental well-being and reduce stress.

- ◆ **Project Management Software.** [11] If one is handing project work, he/she should use project management software like MS Project of Microsoft, or Asana to track the progress.

- ◆ **Time tracking Apps.** Use a time tracking Apps like Toggle or Harvest to see where time is consumed and identify areas where one can be more efficient.

- ◆ **Using available Templates.** It is good practice to prepare templates for commonly used correspondence or for short reply. It saves time of keyboard typing. Templates could be for emailing, letter writing, writing a speech or a book authoring or making Power Point Slides. Use short messaging on multimedia like SMS, WhatsAapp.

Office Automation. [15] Automation is a major time saver for every type of Organization, every Institution, and every Department. It also boosts productivity/efficiency of individuals. Automation of repetitive and manual tasks, will free up employees to focus on more important tasks. Office automation helps getting more businesses done in lesser time. This can lead to increased productivity, happier employees, and cost savings. For instance, auto screening of CVs to short list candidates, will speed up pre-selection process and consequently frees HR officials to undertake other important tasks of HR Department. Automation can lead to increased productivity, happier employees, and even cost savings. Some commonly used methods of time saving through automation are briefly given in following sub-paragraphs:

- ♦ **Automation tools**. These tools may be hardware or software or hardware with embedded software. A tool/equipment like photocopier or heavy duty printer can handle a particular task in seconds, leaving one free to do another creative/important task. Emerging AI tools like Chat GPT, Gemini of Google and Copilot of Microsoft can help in quick web search and collate information on any topic which includes producing software code for any application.

- ♦ **Auto Reply on emails.** Use automation tools like Zapier or IFTTT (If This Then That) to automate repetitive tasks, such as sending emails or scheduling meetings.

- ♦ **Efficient Workflows.** Office automation can connect different software programs and machines, so that information flows smoothly and automatically across the organization. This eliminates the need for manual data entry in multiple places and save lots of time.

Summary. One needs to be better organized and prepare daily/weekly/monthly To-Do lists of tasks. In addition, one should make maximum use of available technologies and automate maximum functions, both at home and at the workplace. The effectiveness of time sharing or multitasking depends on individual factors, task complexity and the specific context. While multitasking may be gainful for certain tasks but it is advisable to focus on one task at a time and minimize distractions to maximize productivity.

Office automation helps in getting more work done in lesser time. One needs to build own time management strategy for becoming more efficient and productive. By adopting good business practices and using right software tools , one can save lots of time to do many other important tasks, Remember, time saving is a judicious use of technologies, automation, skills/tools and various templates. Therefore, one should not get discouraged if one does not see results immediately. Just keep going and trying new strategies and find what works best.

08

TIME AND SPEED RELATIONSHIP

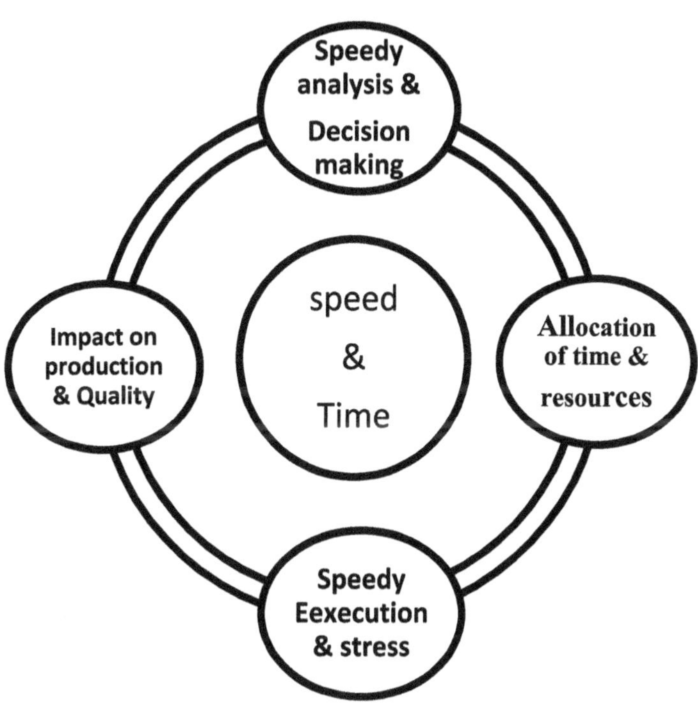

Figure 8.1 Time and Speed Relationship

"It is not the big that eat the small; it is the fast that eat the slow",

– Jason Jennings

In today's fast evolving technologies, rapidly changing our lifestyle, working environment and emerging geo-political unstable environment, it is very important to understand the relationships between time and speed. Speed means faster but not being rash. It is well established that speed during analysis, decision-making, planning, and execution, enhances efficiency and productivity of all professionals and their organizations. We always ask our car driver to speed up because we are getting late for reaching our workplace or attending a seminar/conference or a business meeting. From safety point of view, over-speeding on a road increases risk of accident, heavy strain on the driver and more wear and tear of the vehicle. In fact, if one plans his/her time well, one need not over speed. It is true that faster we go more distance we cover but there is limit related to safety and quality of product/service that we deliver to our customers. As we all know, while travelling or any work done at home or at the workplace, correct speed of our movements/actions is very important. Hence we need to find a right balance between time and speed.

Advantages of Higher Speed. [6] Good old saying *"Slow and Steady Wins the Race"* is not fully applicable today. If we are slow in analyzing customer requirement, decision-making, planning or execution of any assigned project/product, we will miss the deadlines. Some tasks are better done at higher speed, like reading a report or book or data entry. However, tasks like writing a project report or speech for an occasion, requires a more deliberate approach and slower speed. Some major advantages of speed in taking various actions are briefly given below:

♦ Speed acts as a time saver and allows some spare time for free-wheeling and lateral thinking.

♦ Fast analysis of customer requirement, leads to quicker decision making. Likewise, fast decision-making helps in faster planning and scheduling for early start of the project.

- Reduces chance of procrastination *"Pyrolysis though Analysis (PTA)"*.

- Enhances productivity and profitability.

- Assists in effective time management.

Negative Effects of over-speeding. Some negative effects of high speed working which need to be taken care of during Time Management are briefly given below:

- **Burnout of Workforce.** If one constantly makes oneself and his/her team to work at a faster speed, it will cause excessive stress, strain and fatigue. Consequently, it will restrict their ability to focus on their jobs. The workforce will start complaining of ill health and take medical leave more often. This will lower their availability and consequently, there will be drop in productivity.

- **Drop in Quality.** We all remember good old saying *"Hurry spoils the Curry"*. Going fast is helpful as time saver, but rushing through various tasks can lead to more errors and poor quality of workmanship. The product/service of lower quality produced by the workforce will not be acceptable to the customer. Consequently, one has to rework, consume additional time, effort and material to meet Customer Requirement (CR). This will result in cost over-run and also spoil brand name in the market. One may also lose some customers and business partners.

- **Safety of Operating Staff.** Speeding up operations in any production unit, will cause stress and strain resulting in safety risk to the operating staff.

- **Wear and Tear of machinery/tools.** Speeding up operations of machinery could cause strain on certain part of various machines. This stress on machines can result in frequent breakdowns and extra repair of the machinery and tools. This will lower the availability of machines and add to their maintenance cost. Consequently it will lead to drop in production.

♦ **Road safety.** High speed driving a vehicle to reach one's destination, because one did not plan well, can be a safety risk for the driver and other public on the road. Remember fast driving within road safety limits is good but rash driving or crossing road speed limits is dangerous for the driver and others people/ vehicles on the road, Traffic police will stop the driver for over-speeding and he/she will pay heavy fine.

♦ **Drop in Creativity and Innovation.** Today, to be successful in any business whether in domestic or global market, the organization needs frequent innovations. For good innovations, one needs environment which is conducive for creative thinking and evolving quality designs. Speeding through various work processes is not conducive for creative thinking. One needs cool environment for lateral thinking, creative designs, and brain-storming/brain sketching.

Balancing Speed and Time. We all know that fast thinking, analyzing, decision-making, planning and executing result in maximizing productivity of the organization. However, while planning any major task/ project, one should consider it like a marathon race. It is about running smart and not just running fast, get exhausted and drop out of race. We all have seen that marathon race runners do not sprint the entire course. Instead, they would set their pace strategically to achieve the best results. It is therefore important to find the right balance of speed with relation to available time for executing a particular task. Balancing of speed will have following benefits:

- **Boost to Creativity/Innovations.** Working at an optimal speed allows more time to think, brainstorm, evolve new ideas and innovate.

- **Improved Focus.** Taking time to properly plan and prioritize various tasks ensures better concentration/focus on the most important tasks.

- **Improved Quality.** There will be lesser chances of making mistakes, if one is working at optimum speed. Fewer mistakes results in saving time by avoiding rework and fixing them later.

- **Increased Productivity.** Optimum speed will increase productivity and help in meeting deadlines.

- **Less Wear and Tear of Machinery.** There will be less wear and tear of the machinery/tools and will require less repair/maintenance.

- **Personal Safety.** If we are driving at an optimum speed, there will be lesser wear and tear of the vehicle and ensure more personal safety.

- **Safety of Operating Staff.** Working on optimum speed will ensure safety of the workforce.

Speed and Decision-Making Trade off. The relationship between speed and decision making is a trade-off between accuracy and speed in decision making. The ideal decision-making speed depends on the specific situation. The key is to find the right balance between being quick and being thorough. This trade-off is often referred as the ***Speed-Accuracy Trade off***. Some guidelines are given below:

- **Faster Decision Making.** In this situation, we get lesser time to consider various options. This approach can lead to quicker decisions, which may be necessary in urgent situations. However, there's a higher chance of making mistakes due to limited analysis.

- **Slower Decision Making.** Slower time generally leads to better decisions because one can collect more information and weigh the pros and cons of each choice. However, slower decision making will delay the start of the task and meeting deadline.

Summary. Speed has both positive as well as negative effect in our execution of various tasks. Time pressure and stressful situations can impact our judgment and make it harder to think clearly, leading to poorer decision-making. Simple decisions can be made quickly with minimal risk of error. However, complex decisions with many variables often benefit from a slower and more deliberate approach. In this, we can anticipate potential risks and can plan adequate safeguard. People with more experience in a particular area can make faster, more accurate decisions due to familiarity with similar situations.

09

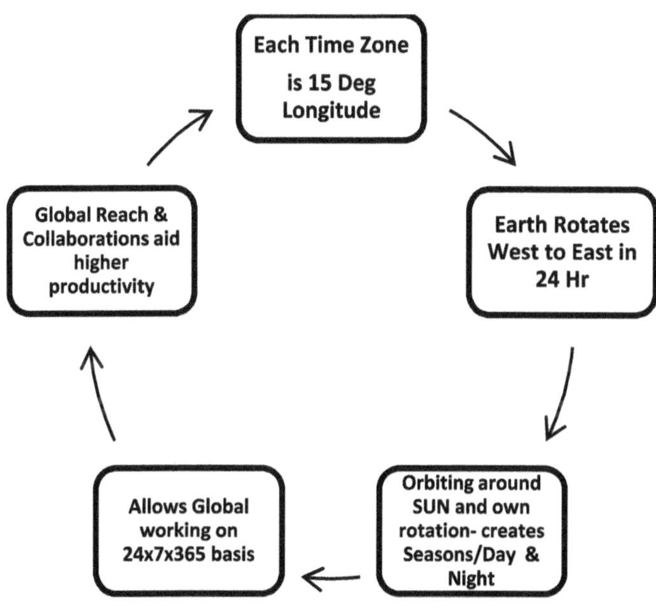

TIME ZONE ADVANTAGE

Figure 9.1 Concept of Time Zone Advantage

"To get over Jet lag, I think a lot of people waste the first few days sleeping in the wrong time zone. Sometimes I take melatonin but at other times a glass of wine will do it".

– Jane Seymour

Time zones relate to the areas on the earth that are divided on the basis of longitudes and that have the same standard time. The Greenwich Meridian has been universally accepted as the starting point that divides the earth's surface into different time zones. Each time zone is 15o longitude wide and the local time is of one hour duration. For effective time management, time zone can be an advantage for 24x7 working and increasing productivity and have more global alliances. By sharing time calendar and video conferencing one can do better scheduling and monitoring of overseas projects.

We all know that our earth planet continuously orbits around the sun and it takes one year (365 days) to complete its one full orbit. This orbit is not circular but elliptical. Depending upon earth's proximity to the sun, we have four seasons – spring, summer, autumn and winter. Our earth is a unique planet which also continuously rotates around its own invisible axis (inclined at 23.5 Degree) and it completes its one rotation in 24 hours. The earth rotates from West to East in anti-clockwise direction which causes Day and Night conditions, depending upon which part of the earth is facing the sun.

With better internet connectivity and efficient mobile communication networks, we can work globally round the clock on a 24x7 basis, without limitation of time zone, For instance, when India has night, USA will have day. Thus we can take advantage of time zone instead of limitation and deploy teams in 2 to 3 shifts and be operational round the clock in the global market. Various Call Centres and back offices are the best examples of gaining from 24x7 working.

Purpose of Time Zones. The purpose of dividing the world into time zones is briefly given below:

- The Greenwich Meridian divides the Earth's surface into different time zones of 15 degrees each. This has been accepted as the starting point. Time zone is the most convenient way of measuring time as it is linked to the movement of the earth, which completes its one revolution in 24 Hours.

♦ The sun is stationary in the middle of its nine planets. Our earth is one of these nine planets which are continuously orbiting around the sun in an elliptical orbit. Because of earth's movement in a fixed orbit around the sun, the sun though stationary, it appears to regularly rise in the East and sets in the West, every day. This is because of the unique configuration of the solar system, where earth keeps revolving around its own axis continuously and simultaneously it keeps orbiting around the sun in an elliptical path.

♦ When the Prime Meridian of Greenwich has the sun at the highest point in the sky, at that time all the places along this meridian will have mid-day or noon.

♦ As the earth completes its one revolution around its own axis from West to East in 24 Hours, all places which are located in the east of Greenwich, will be ahead of Greenwich Time, while those located to the west will be behind Greenwich Time. For instance when it is 1100 (AM) in India, it would be 0700 (AM) in UK.

Calculation of Time Zone. We all know that earth rotates 360° (One full revolution around its own axis) in about 24 hours, which means 15° in one hour or 1° in four minutes. Thus, when it is noon at Greenwich, the time at a place 15° east of Greenwich will be 15 x 4 = 60 minutes, i.e., one hour ahead of Greenwich Time. Likewise, locations at 15° west of Greenwich, the time will be behind Greenwich Time by one hour. However, the local time at the longitude, which generally passes through the middle of a country, is considered to be the standard local time in that country. This standard time is used all over that country for carrying out various types of businesses. However, for carrying out businesses at a global level, there should be compatibility between the standard times of various countries.

Time Zone Division. To facilitate global operations, world has been divided into 24 time zones. These time zones have been created with reference to the Prime Meridian. For instance, USA has six time zones, from West to East namely, Hawaii, Alaska, Pacific, Mountain, Central and Eastern. Russia being the largest country in the world, spreading from the border of Japan in its East and to the Germany in its west, has 11 time zones, which are the maximum in the world. Similarly, Australia has 5 time zones, New Zealand and Indonesia has 2 time zones each, while Japan, India and UK have one time zone each.

Advantages of Time Zones. [10] By adopting suitable business strategies for time zones , we can have following advantages:

- **Cross-Border Collaboration.** Time zone understanding facilitates collaboration with global partnerships.

- **Continuous Productivity.** By leveraging different time zones, organizations can maintain continuous operations and productivity on a 24x7 basis.

- **Faster Response Times.** Timely responses to client enquiries and project updates can be easily achieved across time zones.

- **Expanded Market Reach.** Building good business relationships with clients and business partners in different time zones can open up new business opportunities.

- **Shared Time Calendars.** These tools provide real-time visibility into team members' availability, enabling better scheduling.

Taking Advantage of Time Zones. We can take great advantage in our business operations to enhance productivity and ensure project success by managing time zones effectively. This requires effective communication and coordination among team members, located in different locations, within own country or abroad. Some guidelines for effectively managing time zones are briefly covered in following sub-paragraphs:

- **Cultural Differences.** Respecting different time zones and their local culture/customs is crucial for effective communication and collaboration.

- **Communication Tools.** Utilizing reliable communication tools like email, instant messaging, and project management software is important.

- **Flexible Work Arrangements.** Flexible working hours can accommodate diverse time zone preferences and improve work-life balance.

- **Advance Planning.** One must plan well in advance, indicate milestones, deadlines, and deliverables, taking into account the time zone differences of team members. By planning ahead and setting clear goals, one can minimize delays and ensure project success. This will avoid "Management by Crisis".

- **Establish Suitability of Working hours.** It is important to identify common working hours, when members of all teams could be available for meetings, discussions, and sharing their experiences. This will ensure that everyone is on the same page.

- **Inter Communication Guidelines.** One must set clear communication guidelines to various teams/business partners, which clearly outline preferred modes of communication, response times, and expectations for availability of team members/business partners, across various time zones. This will ensure that all participants are available online, as scheduled by the project manager. One may use online software tools and resources like Time Zone Converters or World Clock Meeting Planner.

♦ **Time Zone Converters**: These can quickly and accurately determine the time difference between dispersed team members. This can ensure that meetings are scheduled at time convenient to all teams.

♦ **Empower Autonomy and Flexibility.** One should encourage autonomy and flexibility among dispersed teams to manage their work schedules in a way that suits their local time zone preferences.

♦ **Shared Calendar.** Maintain a shared calendar that shows each team member's location and availability, based on their local time zone. This can help team leaders to schedule meetings, and video-conferences/ tele-calls in a way that accommodates everyone's time zone preference.

♦ **Video Conferencing.** Video conferencing allows face-to–face communication, regardless of geographic locations of the teams.

♦ **Recording Proceedings of Meetings.** It is useful to do video recording of important conferences, meetings and discussions. This will benefit the team members who may not be able to attend live session due to time zone differences or other administrative reasons. Such team members can use recorded proceedings and stay fully informed and up-to-date on project progress.

♦ **Rotate Meeting Times.** It is important to rotate meeting times so that team members in different time zones have equal opportunities to participate in discussions and decision-making processes. This can also prevent any one group from consistently bearing the burden of inconvenient meeting times.

Summary. By suitably adapting above strategies, one can effectively convert time-zone limitations into time-zone advantage. By effectively managing time zones and implementing efficient communication strategies, organizations can exploit the full potential of global collaboration and achieve higher productivity. Hence, clear communication guidelines to all teams, proactive planning, and flexibility are the keys to converting time zone challenge to functional advantage. That is how people often refer – ***"We are now working in just one Global Village"***. Indeed, we can work round-the-clock (24x7 Basis) and optimize productivity and delivery of products/services. These strategies will facilitate global collaboration/alliances and working across different geographical locations.

10

TIME AND HEALTH RELATIONSHIP

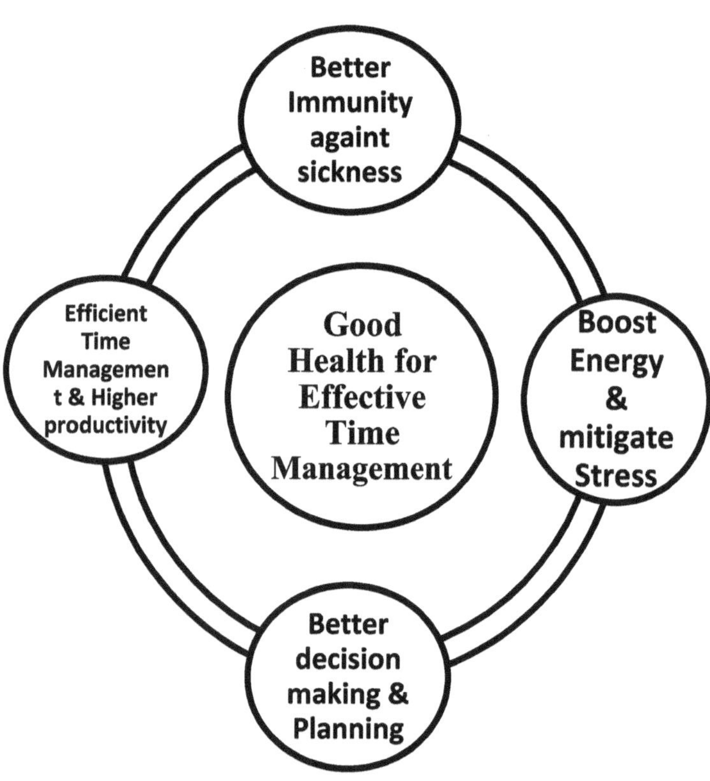

Figure 10.1 Health and Time Relationship

"Time is Money but Health is Wealth."

We all know investing in our health is an investment in our productivity. By keeping good health, one will feel more energized, focused, and capable of achieving his/her goals. They say time is money and one must manage it carefully. We all know every Rupee or Dollar or Pound has value and we carefully do various business transactions, payments and receipts. We also know that every Minute, Hour and Day has great value for various business operations. Those who work on daily wages are paid on hourly basis and those working on contract are paid, say on weekly basis or monthly basis. It is true that to be creative and put in one's full potential at the workplace, one needs good health, else his/her productivity will fall and he/she may often take sick leave to get well.

Health affects Productivity. Good health is the foundation for higher productivity and effective time management. It is true that healthy mind needs healthy body. In turn, it helps to think well, plan well and perform well. Without good health one cannot make good decision and cannot perform well and therefore one cannot earn well. Consequently, one cannot achieve one's life time goals and live under more stress and pressure. One with poor health is unable to cope up with workplace responsibilities and also cannot fully meet family requirements. Continuing with stress and poor health will further spoil one's health. It is important that everyone should consider "Work is Worship" and dedicate to one's job. At the same time, care of the family and own health is also one's major responsibility. Therefore, maintaining good health is essential for ensuring good time management, higher productivity and happy family life.

Stress affects Health. We all have some type of stress but degree/level may differ. Stress is mainly due to change in our life style, faster work flow and need for quicker response during business interaction. Indeed, stress is eating up our available time and we often feel stressed, tired and at times, helpless. A higher level of stress in any form can seriously impact our planning, decision-making and other functioning. It is therefore important to understand symptoms of stress and ways to combat stress, so that we can stay on track, achieve our goal and have happy family life.

Diseases/Ailments due to Persisting Stress. If stress is not controlled in time and allowed to persist over longer time, it can lead to one or more of the following ailments:

- Anxiety Neurosis , Depression , Irritability,

- Body ache, Back ache, Pain in major joints like hip or shoulders,

- Cough and respiratory problems,

- Headache and Eye burning sensation due to sleep disorder,

- Healing of Wounds, Blisters takes longer than normal time.

- High BP, High pulse rate and Heart related ailments,

- Improper functioning of immune system leading to bad cold and infection.

- Indigestion , constipation or loose motions,

- Muscle contraction, Cramps, Headache or Migraine,

- Obesity and Diabetes.

Some common symptom of Stress. To maintain healthy and efficient body one must not allow stress to persist for longer time, since the longer it stays, more harm it can cause to the body. To combat stress one must carefully observe symptoms of stress and then take necessary measures to combat stress. Depending upon nature of job, age, body conditions and family responsibilities, one may show one or more of the following symptoms of stress:

- Fast Breathing and Sweating,

- Feeling butterflies in the stomach and/or loose motions,

- High BP and High Pulse rate,

- Loss of Concentration/focus, nail biting, fingers twisting.

- Muscle Cramps , Backache, Lips turning pale,

Combating Stress. Each person has different response to stress as per his/her age, body conditions, family responsibilities and job overload. It is important to carefully observe stress symptoms and seek proper medication supported by meditation/Yoga exercises. Some common guidelines to combat stress are given below:

- Accept that stress is part of life of everybody and only degree varies. Do not hold others responsible for own stressful life.

- Accept reality of life that one cannot change/control the world and instead, one should try to have self-control.

- Accept responsibility for own actions and decisions and relax. Do not feel helpless and do not play a blame game.

- A simple life and good personal habits are very helpful.

- Take healthy diet which has natural things like green vegetables, fresh fruit, soup, milk, eggs/chicken/fish, dal (Pulses) and rice/roti/bread.

- Delegate certain work to others and don't be "know all". If one thinks that others may not do the task as good he/she can do, one will overload oneself and become a bottle neck in the workflow. Consequently, one will be overwhelmed, since his/her pending tray will pile up.

- Self-discipline is a must. Reaching workplace on time, maintain proper dress code and work enthusiastically will enhance one's personality and impact on others. They will listen to their disciplined leader more willingly and perform better.

- Listening to your favorite songs or music or watching your favorite TV show/movie can be good stress relievers. Likewise, subtle humour, which does not hurt others and laughter can also help,

- Playing at home with the pet and children can help a lot.

- Live within means. They say – *"Cut you coat according to your cloth"*. Stop getting into the rat race and copying/imitating others. Do not try to outpace others.

- Must have a good night sleep. Six to eight hours of good sleep ensures that one is refreshed and ready to perform well every day.

- Good interpersonal skills can enhance one's popularity and boost self-esteem.

- Have positive attitude and adopt policy of- *"forgive and forget"*. Stay cheered up and no sulking.

- Learn to tactfully say NO to distractors, without offending them.

- Listen to own body and do not over stretch. Take short breaks to refresh and recoup energy.

- Manage own personal habits and be disciplined. Be courteous, well-mannered and have positive attitude.

- Meditate daily for at least for 20 minutes. This is a proven way to combat stress. Yoga exercises, if done regularly and properly can keep one fit.

- Take well informed decisions and make good plans, Schedule various tasks as per their priority and capability of team members. Provide adequate resources and time to the team members and hold them responsible.

- Make realistic goals and do not be too optimistic. Adopt SMART (Specific, Measurable, Achievable, Realistic and Time-bound) strategy for goal setting.

- One should be prepared for likely stress due to distraction and be ready to effectively handle various distractors.

- One should organize working table/desk and remove all unwanted files or items which can distract.

- One should manage available time well and avoid crises management.

- One should mind own business and must not walk across to poke his/her nose in others affairs.

- One should not be jealous of other's success. Instead, appreciate good work/success of others and praise them publically.

- Stop being perfectionist and rather deliver on time, even if it is 90% complete but ensure it is operational. In addition, do assure the customer that remaining part will be delivered by a date.

Benefits of Good Health. Good health is the mainstay for effective time management and enhancing productivity. When our bodies and minds are functioning well, we can handle various challenges, focus better on the job-in-hand, and make better use of available time. Some common benefits of good health, as related to productivity are briefly given below:

♦ **Anxiety Minimized.** Anxiety is often caused by stressful life. One become irritable and often plays blame game. If one incorporates relaxation techniques like meditation, Yoga, or deep breathing, the anxiety will be under control.

♦ **Better Sleep.** If you are healthy, you will have good sleep, which is the mantra for ensuring high productivity. Better sleep makes you feel fresh and alert during working hours. An uninterrupted sleep of 6 to 8 hours is crucial every day for efficient cognitive functioning.

♦ **Boost up Energy Levels.** A healthy body is a source of sustained energy. A healthy body allows us to work for longer hours without feeling drained. Indeed, good health helps in maintaining right energy levels which are needed for carrying out various tasks.

♦ **Burnout Prevention.** Good health helps to sustain workload and prevent burnout.

♦ **Combating Stress.** Healthy body, regular physical exercise, yoga/meditation and relaxation techniques can help to combat stress. This way, one stays more efficient and productive.

♦ **Improved Focus and Concentration.** Good health helps us to enhance our cognitive functioning and we can stay focused on job-in-hand.

♦ **Strengthen Immune System.** A healthy person has good immune system which reduces chances of him/her falling sick. Therefore, healthy person can achieve higher availability and productivity.

Maintaining Good Health. Some important suggestions to maintain good health are given below:

♦ **Balanced Diet.** Nourishing one's body with essential nutrients provides the energy needed for good performance. One must have a good mix of proteins, carbohydrates, leafy vegetables and fruit. Taking dry fruit or sweets should be in moderation as even good food taken in excess will act adversely. One may consult a dietician to provide a suitable menu for the day.

- **Eating Habits.** [8]. Remember *"we eat to live and not live to eat"*. Over eating can lead to belly bulging out and sluggishness. Eat well but do not overeat as that will affect digestion and metabolism system. Do not take cold water or cold drink just after a meal. Instead, take something warm like tea or coffee after every major meal. A glass of water may be taken half an hour before or after the meal. Give at least 4 hours gaps between major meals; one should take meal only when one feels hungry. Taking a bowl of soup at lunch and dinner time and a bowl of porridge with milk at break-fast time will keep one healthy and alert.

- **Good Sleep.** Six to eight hours of daily sleep allows the body and mind to recharge and enhance cognitive functioning of our brain. When one is well-rested and has slept well, one is more energetic, more alert, more focused and more productive. Therefore, one should plan for 6-8 hours of sleep daily. It could be 1-2 hours as afternoon nap and 5-6 hours sound sleep at night.

- **Meditation/Yoga.** Guided meditation and Yoga exercises are very useful for stress relieving. Daily 15-20 minutes of meditation will give good rest to one's body and mind. If one does daily meditation one would require lesser medication.

- **Regular Exercise.** Physical activities like brisk walking, jogging and, rope skipping improves blood circulation and reduces stress. Physical activities improve cardiovascular system, enhance cognitive function and one feels energetic.

♦ **Periodic Health Check-up.** Remember good old sayings - ***"Prevention is better than Cure"* and *"A stich in time, saves Nine"*.** Therefore, have periodic healthcare checkup from the family doctor to identify various health issues. Trust the doctor and follow the prescription.

♦ **Do not be a Google Doctor. In today's AI era,** one must not search on Chat GPT/Gemini of Google or Copilot of Microsoft for self- medication as that could have side effects. Do not become Google supported self-doctor and keep munching tablets/capsules like any snack. There can be many side effects affecting other organs.

♦ **Be in touch with Family Doctor.** There are people who take handful of medicines before each meal. This is not the way for keeping good health. Instead, consult the family doctor periodically and seek his/ her advice on Do's and Don'ts, for keeping good health. Trust the doctor and seek his/her advice say every 6 months and follow doctor's prescription religiously. Preventive care helps to identify and address potential health issues in early stage.

♦ **Take short breaks.** Do not keep sitting and working for long hours at a stretch. Instead, get up and move around every 45-60 minutes to avoid burnout. Take a short walk, stretch out, or do some deep breathing exercises say for 10-15 minutes and then return to the work table and resume the job in hand.

Summary. One needs good health to work efficiently else one's productivity will fall and one may often take sick leave to get well. Efficient working requires healthy body to withstand pressure of job and family responsibilities. A healthy leader inspires others to stay healthy and enhance overall productivity. Good 6 to 8 hours of daily sleep is important for number of brain functions and be creative, innovative, and design thinking.

One needs to plan one's life style, eating habits, self-discipline and ability to dispel distractors, which eat up his/her valuable time. Proper sleep allows our brain to rest, create new memories, and help to concentrate and respond quickly to any emerging situation.

11

TIME MEASUREMENT DEVICES AND TOOLS

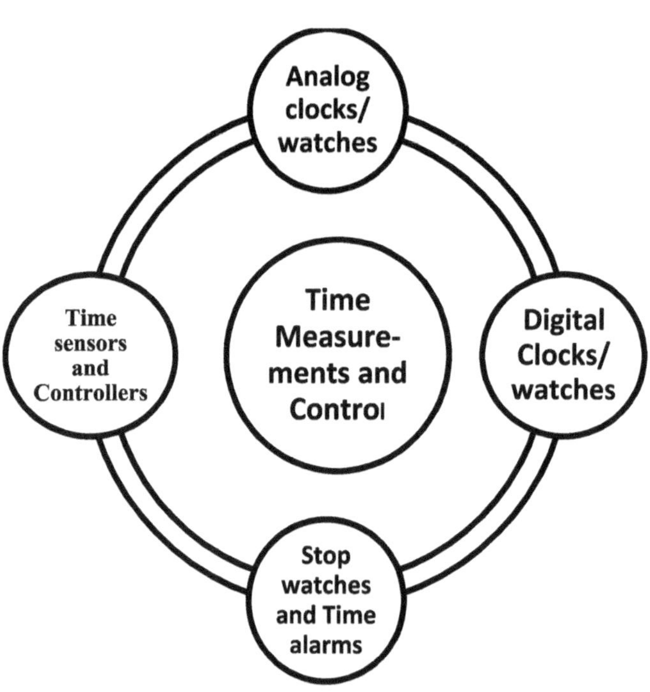

Figure 11.1 – Time Measurement and Control

"I must govern the clock, not be governed by it.

– "Golda Meir

In project management terms, one must plan well before one commences execution of any task. If a project cannot be planned, it need not be undertaken. If a project is planned for execution, it must be regularly monitored through measurements. If progress of a project or a process cannot be measured, it can't be controlled and there is a danger that the project gets derailed and deadline is missed. However, allocating required resources and time blocks to execute a project/task will ensure it is delivered on-time.

To monitor an activity, one has to measure it in terms of time elapsed and progress made. Any delay in project delivery will upset the customer and one will pay extra for working overtime and deploying additional resources to deliver the project.

Time Measuring Instruments/Clocks. There are various types of clocks and watches available to monitor time and track progress of various operations. Some of these clocks/ watches are listed below:

- Analog clocks and watches.
- Digitals clocks and watches.
- Analog/Digital Wall clocks.
- Desk clocks and Computer Screen Clock.
- Wrist Watch with Alarm.
- Stop Watch.
- Time Sensors/controllers.
- Programmable Timers which are based on Microprocessors/Microcontrollers.

Time measurement instruments play a crucial role in effective project management, ensuring all tasks are completed within deadlines and resources are utilized efficiently. Some commonly used instruments/devices/software tools are briefly given in succeeding paragraphs.

Time tracking software tools. Some commonly used software tools for time monitoring are Toggl Track, Harvest, Clockify and Rescue Time. Their main features are:

- Automatic time recording,

- Easy Integration with other project management tools,

- Help in productivity analysis,

- Help in tasks categorization,

Time Sheets. These are simple to use, cost-effective, and widely used time tracking document. Some common features are:

- Customizable formats to suit one's requirement.

- Help in tasks categorization.

- Manual and convenient for time entry.

Card Punch Clocks. These provide a record of working hours. Some common features are:

- Can be integrated with payroll systems.

- Generally used in hourly wage environments.

- Physical device for clocking time in/out of employees.

Activity Trackers. Commonly used activity trackers are Fitbit, Garmin and Apple Watch. Their main features are:

- Easy to wear and carry on person.

- Can provide insights into work patterns and productivity.

- Wearable devices that monitor physical activities.

Project Management Software tools. [11] Some commonly used project management software tools are

– Microsoft Project, Asana, Trello, Basecamp, Their main features are:

- ◆ Built in Task management features.
- ◆ Built-in Time tracking capabilities.
- ◆ Resource allocation/reallocation.

Choosing Time Measurement Instruments/Tools. To have effective control on time and project progress, time measuring/monitoring instruments must be accurate and easy to use. Following points should be considered while choosing a Time Measurement Instrument/tool:

- ◆ **Project Requirements.** Consider the specific needs of the project, such as the nature of work, team size, team locations and desired level of details required.

- ◆ **Affordable Cost.** Evaluate the cost of the tool and any associated fees or subscriptions. It should be affordable by the organization.

- ◆ **Accuracy.** Time measuring tool should provide accurate and reliable time tracking data.

- ◆ **Ease of Use.** Choose a tool that is user friendly and easy for the team to use.

- ◆ **Easy to Integrate.** Select the tool that can easily integrate with other project management tools, which are already in use in the organization.

Summary. For good quality assurance and meeting deadlines, one needs time measuring instruments/software tools which are efficient, accurate and are easy to use by the team. For quality assurance of the product/service, one needs to carry out close monitoring and do in- process control. By selecting an appropriate time measurement instrument/ tool, one can effectively monitor and control project activity, improve efficiency, and ensure successful project completion. This will build confidence among team members and also create good name in the market and among business partners.

12

TIME MANAGEMENT TECHNIQUES AND STRATEGIES

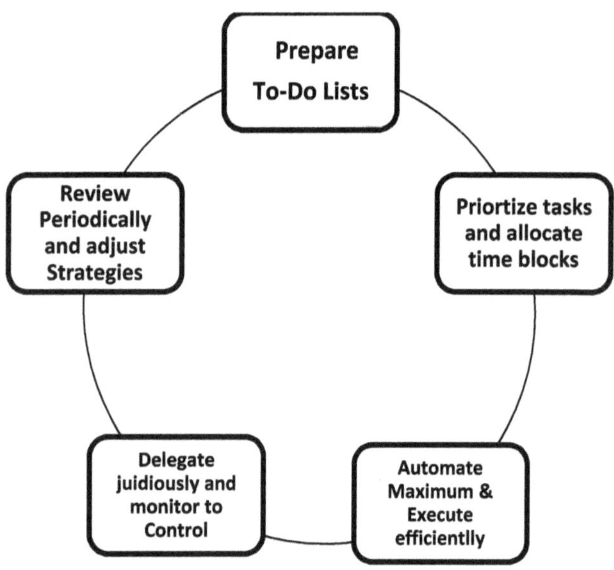

Figure 12.1 Time Management Techniques and Strategies

"The key to success is not in managing time, but in managing your energy. If you manage your energy, you will manage your time."

– Jim Rohn

Time is the most valuable and critical asset but limited to just 24 hours a day. Out of this time one may get just 8 to 10 hours at work place, 1 to 2 hours for commuting from home to workplace and 3-4 hours for the family and other household chores. Time management is both an art and technique for balancing times related to daily routine activities at home, commuting to the workplace and job activities at the workplace. However, to rise in career and living a quality life, amidst today's uncertain/chaotic world, one needs to manage time well.

It is well established that effective time management is crucial for ensuring higher productivity and greater success of any organization, which may relate to any field like Processing Industry, Manufacturing, Road Transportation, Logistics, Aviation, Railways, Shipping, Healthcare, Agriculture and Education. Likewise, effective management of time is equally important for any individual working in any organization.

Remember, effective time management is not about doing more and selling more. Instead, it is about doing the right things, on-time and efficiently. Thus, effective time management is crucial for achieving higher productivity and good personal growth.

Strategies for Effective Time Management. [9] By combining self-awareness and understanding capabilities of the team, one can optimize overall productivity and achieve own as well as organizational goals. The strategies for effective time management will relate to nature of job and position of the person in the organization. Most of us feel quite fresh and energetic in the morning or after we have taken good sleep. Therefore, one should identify the most challenging or complex task to be undertaken first thing in the morning, since that is prime time. Some suggested strategies for effective time management are briefly given below:

- **Set SMART Goals.** One should start by defining one's goals as what he/she wants to achieve in short terms (3-5 years) and Long terms (15-30 years). One should set simple and clear goals which follow SMART approach- Specific (S), Measurable (M), Achievable (A), Relevant (R) and Time-bound (T).

- **Prepare To-Do Lists.** One should carefully prepare "To-Do" lists of tasks to be done within a Day, within a Week, within a Month or within a Quarter.

- **Prioritization Techniques.** One should quickly examine every To-Do list and allocate priorities for daily, weekly and monthly load for the team. Most commonly, used techniques for prioritizing are briefly given below:

  - **ABCDE Method.** Assign a letter to each task based on its importance. A- for the most crucial/ important tasks, B- for important tasks, C- for less important tasks, D- for delegating tasks and E- for tasks to be eliminated.

  - **Eisenhower Matrix.** Categorize tasks into four quadrants. Put Urgent and important tasks in quadrant 1, Important but Not Urgent in quadrant 2, Urgent but not Important in quadrant 3 and Neither Urgent nor Important tasks, in quadrant 4. One should focus on tasks in the first quadrant.

- **Work Efficiently.** A leader and his/her team must be well knit to work efficiently, using available technologies and material resources. One must understand the potential and use of various time-management software tools, which are available in the open market.

- **Ensure effective Communication.** Maintain unambiguous and effective communication with the team to avoid misunderstandings and ensure everyone is aligned to the common goal.

- **Organize Better.** One needs to remove all unwanted articles/material from the work desk. Keep only those items, which one needs to immediately carry out priority tasks. Do not let things pile up in the in-tray/pending tray.

- **Flexible Planning for Emergent task.** While planning one's daily work schedule, one should have some cushion to suspend operations on main job on hand and undertake any small but very important job. After completion of that small and urgent task, one should resume the main task and catch up with timeline. Salient points to be kept in mind are given below:

  - Break down large jobs into smaller and manageable jobs.

  - Create a detailed plan.

  - Set clear and achievable goals.

  - Write down the steps required to achieve goals and allocate adequate time for each.

  - Periodically review which approach is working fine and which is not. Make adjustments as needed.

  - One should be flexible and willing to modify one's approach, if it is not giving desired results.

- **Time Blocking.** Allocate specific blocks of time say 30-45 minutes each for different tasks. This helps to maintain focus and prevent distractions.

- **Create a Daily Schedule.** One should plan the day by allocating time blocks of say 30-45 minutes each for various tasks.

- **Time Sharing.** Adopting of this technique will result in time saving and giving higher throughput. However, application of time sharing should be done selectively.

- **Multi-Tasking.** As the name suggests multi-tasking means attending to more than one job at the same time. In this case, one may suspend the job in hand and attend to the new job, which may be of higher priority. After completing high priority job, one resumes the suspended job and carries on. Multi-tasking can gainfully use idle time and maximize the output. However, sometimes multi-tasking is distractor and lowers productivity.

- **Time Tracking.** Use software tools to monitor how one spends one's time and identify areas for improvement. Likewise, keep a track of time utilized by the team. It is useful to carry out in-process correction now instead of doing rework at a belated stage.

- **Time Distractors Management.** One must check what all are the unnecessary activities called time-killers/distractors/destroyers. If these distractors are not managed properly, these will eat up one's time and one will always be short of time and feel overloaded/overwhelmed. More on this has been covered in chapter 6. Some suggestions to combat distractors are given bellow:

  - Turn off notifications and close unnecessary tabs/links appearing on the workstation.

  - One should find a quiet environment and do not allow people just to walk in, when one is doing a serious work.

  - Use website blockers to limit access to time-wasting websites.

- **Take Regular Breaks**. Short breaks reduce stress/ fatigue, make one relax and improve productivity. One may work vigorously say for 45 minutes, then take a short break of say 5- 10 minutes to get refreshed and energetic. After working says for 2- 3 hours, one many take a longer break of 15 – 30 minutes.

- **Delegate Judiciously**. It is important to delegate some tasks to others for greater productivity. One should not be "Know-all" and keep everything in own in- tray. Instead, train the team to undertake bigger roles and delegate certain tasks to team members as per their capability and capacity. This way, one can have some free time for creative thinking or doing more urgent tasks.

- **Setting Boundaries.** Set boundaries for time to be spent at home and at the workplace. One should adhere to these limits and let these be known at the workplace and at home.

- **Learn when to Say No.** Be bold and say "No" to time-wasting people/tasks. Do not seek popularity/ praise by accepting any task/job which comes at any unscheduled time. One must avoid overcommitting when one and his/her team is already having enough on their hand. Be tactful and firm to say NO.

- **Continuous Learning.** One should ensure that he/she does continuous learning of new skills and stay updated. In addition, one must encourage a culture of learning and development within the team and provide them resources and funds.

- **Discipline.** Self-discipline and discipline among team members is the basic requirement to achieve higher productivity. Reaching and leaving the workplace on-time by the leader motivates others to follow.

- **Stay Healthy and fit**. One must ensure to get enough sleep, eat healthy food, and do physical exercises regularly to maintain good health. Without good health one cannot perform well.

Time Discipline Benefits. Time discipline must apply at all levels, as it helps in greater availability of workforce and enhance overall productivity. This includes aspects like arriving on time, staying focused while working at the workplace and adhering to break schedules. The example of good discipline should start from the top so that lower down everybody follows this as a work culture. How time discipline contributes to improve productivity at the workplace and quality of family life is briefly given below:

- **Controls time breaks.** Taking short breaks at designated times allows one to recharge and avoid burnout. Returning from breaks on time ensures that one does not cut into his/her productive periods of his/her job.

- **Demonstrates Leadership.** On-time arriving and departing from one's workplace, demonstrates one's professionalism and respect for colleagues and project deadlines. The team members will get inspired and follow habits and discipline standards of their leader.

- **Improves Focus and Quality.** Knowing one has a dedicated time block for the allotted work, motivates one to stay focused and avoid distractions. This leads to higher concentration and better quality work output.

- **Motivates. Following a** consistent work schedule, makes one more time consciousness and his/her body and mind get fully aligned to the deadlines. This helps one to stay motivated and maintain enthusiasm throughout the day.

- **Reduces Time Wastage.** Sticking to a scheduled time table minimizes unproductive activities like unnecessary breaks or getting sidetracked during working hours.

Summary. One should work hard to learn new skills to outshine in one's team/organization and gain popularity. For this, one needs to do regular SWOT analysis and continuously learning newer technologies and processes to stay ahead. Minimize distractions like social media interaction, excessive emails, unscheduled visitors and unnecessary meetings.

By suitably adapting above strategies, one can take control of 'one's time, enhance productivity and create a more fulfilling and harmonious home life. It is important for one to manage stress and stay fit to perform his/her duties to the fullest. Time management strategies should change with availability of emerging technologies and business processes. Hence one should regularly review one's time management strategies and make appropriate adjustments.

13

TIME SHARING AND MULTI-TASKING

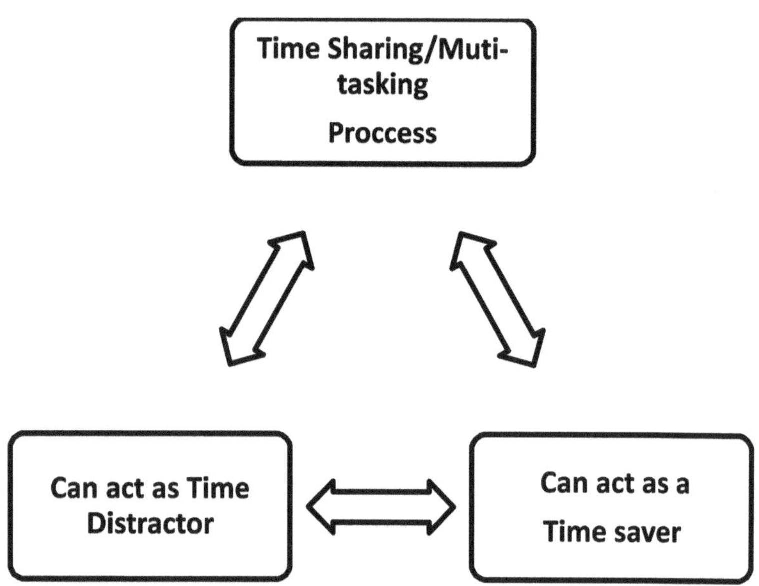

Figure 13.1, Time Sharing/Multi-tasking as a Saver/Distractor

"You can do two things at once, but you can't focus effectively on two things at once."

– Gary Keller.

In our daily life we often resort to Time sharing/Multi-tasking while executing various tasks whether at home or at workplace. A task may be executed manually, electronically, or by using electro-mechanical equipment. Time sharing is related to assigning a fixed time slice to more than one task, such that smaller job is completed faster while other jobs are also in progress. It is like Round Robin techniques used in computer Operating System (OS) for multi-programming environment. Time sharing helps in overall time saving and enhancing productivity. Multi-tasking is related to doing multiple jobs concurrently and switching between jobs. However, it has to be used discreetly, since too much multi-tasking will cause time fragmentation, disturb concentration and reduce overall productivity.

In real life, both time-sharing and multi-tasking are used inter-changeably. Although both time-sharing and multi-tasking are techniques to handle multiple tasks, yet they differ subtly in their approach and impact on time management. Actually, time-sharing and multi-tasking act as two sides of a coin. Their major benefits and drawbacks are briefly covered in succeeding paragraphs:

Time Sharing.[16]

♦ **Small Jobs finish faster.** In time sharing, one allocates same time slice for each task. One works on one task for a set period, then switches to the next, and so on. In this process smaller task gets completed faster. Its focus is on sequential completion of all tasks in the To-Do list.

♦ **Reduces Stress and Anxiety,** It minimizes the mental burden of juggling multiple tasks and contextual switching of jobs as it happens in case of multi-tasking.

♦ **Improves Focus and Productivity.** Time sharing improves focus and productivity due to dedicated undivided attention to each task.

- **Enhance the Quality of Work**. It helps in producing higher-quality results with fewer errors.

Multi-tasking. If one has several small and unrelated tasks, multi-tasking might be efficient, like one could answer emails while waiting for a download to complete. It acts both as time saver and as a time distractor as given below:

- **As a time saver**

    - **Simultaneous handling of tasks**. Multi-tasking involves attempting to work on multiple tasks simultaneously. It resorts to frequent switching between tasks with a view to use idle time and increase productivity.

    - **Multi-tasking maintains momentum.** In multi-tasking, switching between tasks can prevent boredom and helps one to stay active throughout the day.

- **As a Distractor.**

    - **Multi-tasking reduces focus.** Continuous switching of tasks can result in poor attention, since it becomes harder to focus on any one task. This can lead to errors, resulting in poor quality and rework at own extra cost.

    - **Increases mental stress.** The mental effort required to continuously switch tasks and keeping track of multiple tasks can be stressful. This will adversely affect the overall productivity.

    - **Increases time to complete tasks.** Multi-tasking can lead to errors, delays, and ultimately waste more time than it saves.

Effective Time Management Strategy. The key to effective time management is to find a strategy that suits individual needs and helps one to work efficiently and productively. By focusing on one task at a time, multi-tasking might be appealing but time sharing is generally considered a more effective time management strategy,

The impact of time sharing or multi-tasking on productivity has many views. One view is that multi-tasking can enhance productivity by allowing individuals to efficiently switch between tasks and utilize idle time effectively. Likewise, multi-tasking can be beneficial in certain situations, such as dealing with repetitive or low-complexity tasks. Yet another view is that multi-tasking can hinder productivity. The human brain is not designed to efficiently switch between tasks, and constant context switching can lead to reduced focus, increased errors, and decreased overall performance. Hence, time sharing/multi-tasking has to be done in certain circumstances and not as a routine.

Summary. It is important to note that the best approach for adopting time sharing or multi-tasking strategy can vary depending on individual preferences, availability of resources and the nature of the tasks involved. Some people may find that a hybrid approach, combining elements of time sharing and multi-tasking, works best for them. By intelligently employing time sharing/multi-tasking strategy, one can stay more focused and productive.

14

EFFECTIVE TIME MANAGEMENT AT WORKPLACE

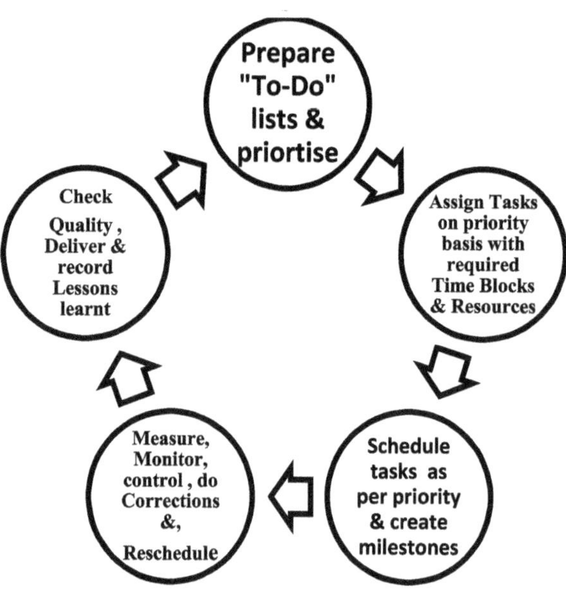

Fig 14.1 Time Management in an Organization -Typical Cycle

"Productivity is never an accident. It is always the result of a commitment to excellence, intelligent planning and focused effort".

– Paul j. Meyer

Effective Time Management (ETM) at the workplace is linked to type and size of the organization, which could be Small, Medium, Large, Domestic, Multinational (MNC) or Global organization. Likewise, ETM is also related to the structure of the organization which could be hierarchical, matrix, network or flat. The organization may relate to any field say Healthcare, Education , Agriculture, Construction, Transportation, Manufacturing, Processing industry (Oil and Chemical, Food/and Drinks or Cement or Fertilizer), Shipping, Government department like Finance, Defence , Railways, Aviation or Research Labs. Therefore, management of time will relate to nature of organization, nature of job and position/responsibility of the person in the organization. However, some basic principles for ETM are common to all organizations whether run by the government or by the private parties or a combination (Public, Private Partnership - PPP). Time management of self-employed and working from home or a small entrepreneur is a different ball game, since they have to do lot of multi-tasking, time sharing and often stretch their working beyond normal working hours.

Workplace Types. You could be working as a Team Member, Team Leader, Delivery Manager, Product Design Engineer, Assembly Line Supervisor, Quality Tester, Receipt and Dispatch (R&D) Manager, Project Manager or CTO/CEO. While working in on-site projects, it could be open space at sites for Construction of Building/Malls/Housing complexes, Survey and Exploration, Mining, Construction of Dams, Roads, Bridges and Tunnels. If one is in marketing team, he/she could be mostly travelling, and interacting with existing/future customers. While in other jobs like Manufacturing, Banking, Software Company, Healthcare, Education, Research Labs, one could be working in a closed space. This type of job could be operating in a hall with many professionals having seats and workstations/lap tops to carry out their jobs. It could also be a long hall for production assembly-line, quality testing and dispatch in a manufacturing plant. In all these places, one needs to be well organized. One should stay focused on the job and strictly follow work culture, ethos and discipline of the organization.

Time Availability. Daily, we all just get 24 hours, which includes day and night. Out of these 24 hours, we spend say 3-4 hours with family, have 6-8 hours of sleep, 1-2 hours of morning chores and healthcare exercises and 1-2 hours commuting to workplace. Thus, we get just 8-10 hours at the work place to complete our daily assigned tasks. Hence, we need proper planning for management of our available time in an effective manner. Depending upon type, size and structure of the organization/institution and nature of job, there are various strategies/techniques to manage one's time at the workplace. Some commonly used strategies are briefly given in succeeding paragraphs.

General principles of Time Management. General principles of time management as relevant to any workplace are given below:

- ◆ **Planning.** Planning is the most important step for any professional/team leader/manager in any organization. He/She should examine priority list of tasks and available resources to judiciously allocate time blocks and required resources. Planning is not an art but a process to organize all available resources, schedule various tasks and allocate time blocks indicating start date and time as well as finish date and time.

- ◆ **Prepare daily Schedule**. One should schedule various tasks and per their priorities, allocating specific time slots for each task. One should build in some buffer time for unexpected events, like a representative from customer or vendor showing up unexpectedly.

- **Monitoring and Control.** Once the jobs/tasks are scheduled, these must have regular monitoring and control to keep events on track. It is rightly said, "What cannot be planned need not be undertaken and what is undertaken for execution should be monitored and controlled regularly". Otherwise, it could lead to time and cost over-runs. A successful manager will carry out in–process control by closely monitoring the progress and readjust resources to meet deadlines.

- **Focused Working.** Earmark specific periods in a day/week for very important tasks as these require working without any distraction. One should turn off notifications on laptop and silence phone during this time. This will improve one's efficiency and productivity.

- **Minimize Interruptions**: Inform colleagues and family members about your focused working time and politely decline unnecessary meetings or conversations during that period.

- **Learn When and How to say NO.** Do not hesitate to politely decline additional tasks, if your plate is already full. Likewise, do not leave task at hand to accommodate unscheduled visitor. One should explain one's workload/occupancy and suggest alternative solutions or time.

- **De-clutter your workspace.** A messy work table/desk indicates a messy and cluttered mind. One must keep one's workspace clear of all items like flowerpots, books, files, equipment or instruments which can cause distractions. One should keep on the work table, only essential items/equipment, tools and documents which one needs, readily available.

- **Manage Distractions**. Turn off notifications and commercial advertisements which pop up on the laptop/smart phone to divert one's attention. One should close unnecessary browser tabs and block unwanted websites. Some of these use persistent agent and tempt one to suspend his/her job in-process and pay attention to other website.

- **Have short Breaks**. To stay fit during whole day, one should step away from work table/desk regularly, say every 45 minutes and go for short (say 5-10 minutes) walk and stretch out, or have some coffee to freshen up. This can help to refocus and return with renewed energy.

- **Health Care**. They rightly say, ***"Time is Money but Health is Wealth"***. Healthy person can be more productive and take extra load when needed. It is true that one will feel fresh and energetic, if one has rested well. Therefore, one must have lifestyle that ensures enough sleep of 6-8 hours, eating nutritious meals, and doing regular physical exercise in a Gym or have long brisk walk.

- **Sense of Accomplishment**. It is ever true- ***"Nothing succeeds like Success"***. Therefore, it is important to feel happy and energetic when one has spent the day as planned,

- **Invest Time and Funds**. One should invest time and money for self-improvement and skill development of the team. This will make one more efficient in performing one's duties. Always stay up-to-date in using new business processes, new quality standards and follow rules/regulations. This will enhance one's popularity within the team/organization and respect from the customers and business partners.

Strategies for Effective Time Management. Effective time management is crucial for enhancing productivity and achieving greater success. Time management is important both for an individual professional and for an organization. Remember, time management is not about doing more but rather about doing the right things, on-time and efficiently. A judicious mix of following strategies can help for optimum use of available time:

- **Goal Setting.** It is important to set realistic and achievable goals. One should not overwhelm oneself with endless To-Do lists. Follow the popular principle of SMART goals (S-Specific, M- Measureable, A- Achievable, R- Relevant and T- Time-Bound). One must be clear about one's goals as what he/she wants to achieve in short terms (3-5 years) and Long terms (10-20 years) of the chosen career.

- **Preparing To-Do lists.** It is very important to prepare To-Do lists of tasks to be done within a day, a week and a month. These To-Do lists should take care of work-In-Progress (WIP) as well as new jobs/tasks being offered.

- **Prioritize Tasks.** Once To-Do lists of tasks are ready, next important action is to prioritize the tasks without any bias. Use time management techniques like the Eisenhower Matrix to categorize tasks. One must differentiate between most urgent, urgent, important and lesser important tasks. Tackle the most urgent task first, and consider delegating or re-scheduling less important tasks.

- **Use Time Blocking.** Time block is a very convenient tool for planning and monitoring of any project. One may create time blocks say of 40 -45 minutes, in which a good amount of work could be done. Allocate specific blocks of time for different tasks. This helps to maintain focus and prevent distraction.

- **Create a Daily Schedule.** Plan the day by allocating time blocks for various tasks. Use tools like time blocking to organize the schedule. Keep in mind capacity and capability of the team members.

- **Flexibility for Emergent task.** While planning daily work schedule, one should have some cushion to suspend operations on main job and undertake any small but very important job. After completion of emergent job, one should resume the main task.

- **Have few Meetings.**

  - Schedule meetings only when necessary.

  - Keep meetings focused and short.

  - Use tools like video conferencing to reduce travel time.

- **Take Regular short Breaks.** Planned short breaks improve productivity. One may work for 45 minutes then take a 5-10 minutes break to get refreshed and reenergized.

- **Open Seating.** One should do away with work cabins for managers and have everyone working in open space. This will minimize loitering around and gasping in close cabins. Open seating is now quite common in banks and IT sectors. It has been found very effective.

- **Realistic Deadlines.** If one does not set deadlines, one could be having slippages in completing a given task and earn poor impression from the customers and business partners.

- **Handle Distractors Firmly.** Avoid all types of time distractions and learn the art of saying tactfully but firmly NO to unscheduled visitors.

- **Communicate Effectively.** One must be clear while giving instructions to the team. There should not be any doubt or misunderstanding in the minds of the recipients.

- **Stay focused on the job in hand.** Do not accept interruptions by unscheduled visitors. Concentrate on the job in hand and stay focused.

- **Keep Paper Work under control.** Ensure that your in-tray has minimum files. Throw away junk documents in the dustbin.

- **No pending work.** Do not let pending work pile up. Just Do it as per priorities.

- **Proper Indexing and Filing.** Do proper indexing and filing of important documents and rest should be shredded or discarded in the dustbin

- **Utilizing Slack hour.** If you have some slack/free time, you may do the following:

  Deal with pending emails.

  - Go through short notes taken in meetings/conferences.

  - Index and Archive files both in physical form as well as e-file on Google drive or One Drive of Microsoft or an external disk drive.

  - Make all pending tele calls/WhatsApps messages.

  - Read pending reports and make notes for action,

  - Read professional journal/News Letter/Book to stay updated.

  - For relaxation, one may solve Crossword Puzzle/Sudoku puzzle or play chess or a short video game.

  - Walking and Thinking. Go for a leisure walk and let your mind fly. It helps in free thinking and idea generation.

- **Use Time Management Tools.**

  - Utilize productivity apps and calendars to organize your schedule.

♦   Set reminders and alarms to stay on track.

Review Strategies and Improve. One should regularly review one's time management strategies and identify the areas for improvement.

Summary. Remember, Time Management is not one shot solution but a continuous process of experimenting ideas and improving. Therefore, one should experiment different strategies and find out what suits best for him/her. Based on one's personal experience and judgment, one should adjust one's strategies. One should take help from colleagues or supervisors, if one is struggling with some complex task. It is very important to focus on priority tasks and tactfully say NO to distractors and unscheduled tasks and visitors.

Time is the most critical resource and one needs to have full control on it. This is very necessary since one is accountable for on-time completion of task assigned by his/her seniors. Proper discipline and decorum at the workplace must be maintained and never go for accepting mediocre work just for cheap popularity. A leader should be hard-task-master but caring for his/her team, seniors and customers. There is no universal strategy "One Fit All". One needs to experiment with different techniques to find what works best for him/her. By implementing appropriate strategies, one can enhance own productivity, reduce stress, and achieve a better work-life balance.

15

EFFECTIVE TIME MANAGEMENT AT HOME

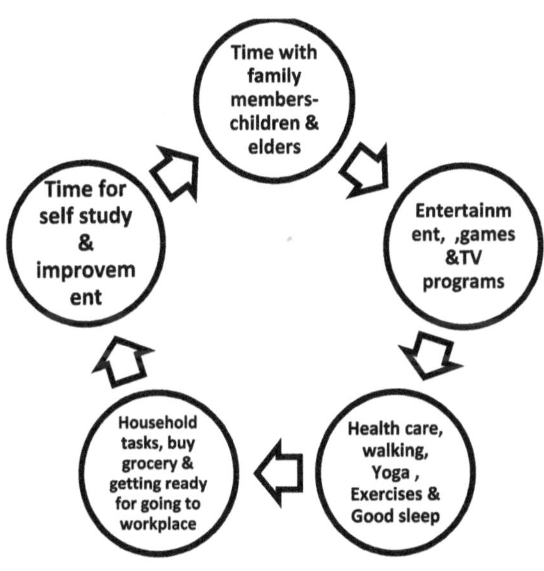

Figure 15.1. Time Managing for Home Environment

"You get to decide where your time goes. You can either spend it moving forward or you can spend it putting out fires, you decide."

– Tony Morgan

It is very important to pay maximum attention to one's job at work-place. It is equally important to pay good attention for well-being of the family. Remember, one cannot perform to one's full potential if there is no peace at home. The family could be just oneself and spouse or one could have children, old parents and grandparents staying in one home. While one is away to the workplace, those left at home keep waiting whole day, for their dear one to come back home and spend time with them. It is therefore, very important to spare adequate time for them and make them happy every day. Some people are workaholic and they spend more time at the workplace and even carry some pending work to do at their homes. This can cause uneasiness in the family, since they are not getting their expected time from their dear one.

Similarly, one will remain mentally disturbed if some members of the family are anguished, feeling that they are being neglected. Therefore, one needs to evolve a good strategy for spending sufficient time with family members, meet their requirements and keep them happy. It is natural that some family may be staying in a village, in a small town, in a big city or in a cosmopolitan city and they will have different requirements. Likewise, commute time could be different as per location, distance and conditions of the route. Some basic guidelines for effective time management at home are briefly covered in succeeding paragraphs. These may be modified to suit one's family environment.

Automation. Use maximum household appliances which have timer control. These could be Washing Machine/Dryer, Dish washer, Bread Toaster, Food Warmer/Microwave/Oven, Water sprinkler for garden/lawn or a Robot for floor cleaning.

Create a Daily Schedule of Activities. It may include tasks like helping children in doing their school homework, helping in kitchen, morning chores, gardening, lawn/plant watering, meals preparation, playing with kids and entertaining elders in the house, local shopping and relaxation. Some useful actions points are given below:

- Prioritize tasks and allocate specific time slots for each task.

- If affordable, engage a maid/servant for helping in kitchen work and house cleaning.

- Divide some tasks among family members, as per their availability.

- Be realistic and flexible. One should have cushion to accommodate some urgent event.

- Engage an agency or a person to do weekly tasks like lawn mowing.

Earmark Work place. This is one's mini workplace within the house and one should make it conducive to comfortable and efficient working. Some guidelines are given below:

- One needs to concentrate on work/study or freewheeling for idea generation. There should be minimum distraction/interruptions from others. Find a quiet place where family members do not just walk in.

- Keep a good work table with drawers and a comfortable revolving and well cushioned chair.

- Keep the workplace well organized, well lighted and clutter free.

- Keep the workplace well equipped and necessary items handy.

- It should have good Broad Band connectivity, good WIFI router, Power back up, Workstation/Workbook with authorized latest Window office software , Adobe PDF Reader,

- Have good quality Printer cum Scanner and stationery.

♦ It should have good quality video camera, mouse pad. Microphone and speakers.

Set Boundaries.

♦ Establish clear boundaries between work and personal time and be it known to the family members.

♦ Do not bring files from the workplace to work at home.

♦ Avoid checking work emails or taking work calls during personal time as that is meant for family members.

♦ One should inform one's availability to colleagues and friends.

Minimize Distractions.

♦ Turn off notifications on mobile phone and computer, during focused work time.

♦ Tell people at workplace not to ring you at home until it is emergent.

♦ Use website blockers to limit access to social media and other distractions.

Health Care. [8] We all know "Heath is Wealth ". To perform one's duties efficiently at the workplace and at home, you need to be 100% fit physically as well as mentally. If your health is not good, you will feel tired, and lazy, which will impact your performance and productivity of the organization. Therefore, it is one's personal responsibility to take care and keep oneself fit. Some basic guidelines for fitness are briefly given below:

♦ **Good Sleep.** One should prioritize one's sleep and regulate to daily sleep at the same time, say 1-2 hours after dinner. One must ensure that one gets 5-6 hours uninterrupted sleep. When one gets up after good sleep, one will feel fresh and energetic to carry out any task.

♦ **Food**. Avoid market supplied fast food. Instead, eat healthy home cooked food with a gap of 4 to 5 hours between meals,

♦ **Entertainmen**t. One should plan some time for hobbies and entertainment activities as per his/her taste. It is important to involve family members and enjoy their company.

♦ **Stress Reliever**. Doing Morning Prayers and Meditation can help to reduce stress. In this regard, playing with children or pet can also help.

♦ **Walking is best**. Morning/evening walk is very helpful. It could be brisk walk for 5 to 6 Km in any nearby park.

♦ **Gym/Yoga**. Some Yoga and physical exercises in a nearby Gym can keep one fit.

♦ **Lawn mowing.** Lawn mowing is required only if one has lawn outside the house. This activity serves both as an exercise and beautifying lawn/mini garden. One could even outsource it, since lawn mowing is bit hard and is done once a week.

♦ **Watering lawn and plants.** One can automate lawn watering using timer fitted sprinklers. These come up and go down automatically as per preset timing.

♦ **Fast getting ready and having breakfast.** It gives good feeling to have breakfast with family members on the dining table.

♦ **Leaving home on time.** It is important to collect all needed items, pack the bag and take out the vehicle from the garage or call a taxi for going to the Metro

Railway Station or Bus stand. It could also be walking up to a pick up point of the Chartered Bus.

♦ **Arriving home on time.** It is good to reach home at the expected time and greet people at home. Have tea together and relax. It may be watching a match or movie on the TV.

♦ **Delegation.** Some tasks could be distributed among family members and even children, as they can do it quickly and cheerfully.

Summary. Remember, a house becomes a home where the family lives in happily. However, if there are quarrels, unhappiness and tension in the home, one cannot do well at the workplace. It is also important that home should not be treated as a guest house to stay for the night and go away in the morning. We are human and it is necessary to have love, jokes and fun together.

A person, who leaves home in the morning in a huff and in an agitated mood, will be sulking during commuting and remain worried at the workplace, thinking as what could be happening at home, Consequently, one's performance will come down since one cannot focus on the job. Similarly, if one returns home fully exhausted and rush to the bed room to watch TV without greeting family members, they will be unhappy and feel neglected. It is universally well established that to perform well at the workplace one must lead a happy family life.

16

BALANCING TIME BETWEEN WORKPLACE AND HOME

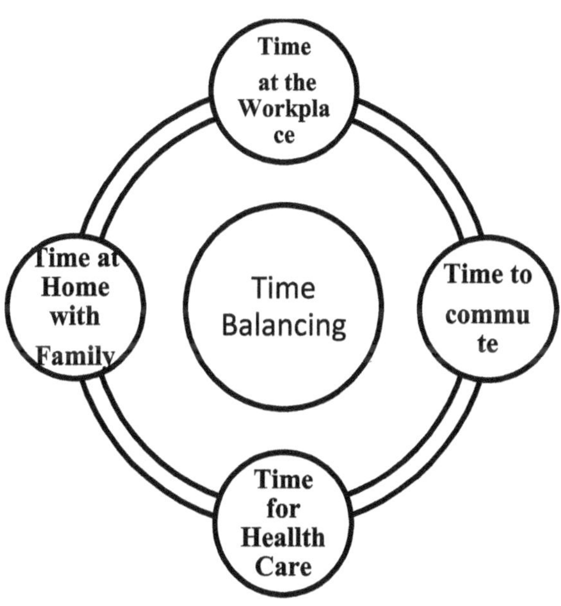

Figure 16.1 Balancing daily Time Utilization

"Planning and prioritizing assures success and wellbeing, lack of planning leads to confusion, stress, drop in productivity, missing deadlines and unhappy family life".

– Anonymous

A number of professionals are over devoted to their job and they are often called workaholic. They do not devote sufficient time for caring their family members who wait whole day for their dear one to return and sit/play/chat with them. Such professionals also do not care for their own health and often feel tired, stressed out and frequently take sick leave. There are many cases of extreme workaholics who work late at the workplace and some even carry work from their workplace to their home. It is well established that to work with one's full potential, one should be happy at home else, one feels nagged by family members. It is also true that finding a balance between job and family is a personal effort and requires some trial and error to find what works best. In all cases, one needs to be more understanding, responsible and patient to make adjustments and lead a happy work-family life.

Strategies for Time Balancing. Irrespective of the work environment and duties at the workplace and family size, whether small or large, one has a major role to play for success in one's career and happiness at home. To lead a happy and successful life in present day scenario of global uncertainty and cut-throat market, some professionals work overtime and overload themselves to earn a bit more. One must realize that we are human and not robots to work tirelessly around the clock. We need to have proper balance between times spent at the workplace, in commuting to the workplace, for healthcare and to support our family.

Indeed, balancing time between one's job and family is a very challenging job. However, with effective time management, positive attitude and clear communication among family members, a harmonious atmosphere can be created to make house a happy home. Some guidelines to evolve a good time balance between work and home life are given in succeeding paragraphs.

- ◆ **Job Type and Working Environment.** The nature of job and one's position in the organization could be different. For instance, one could be doing a job related to office work/chair-bound, site construction, manufacturing, logistics, transportation, aviation, shipping, marketing, healthcare and education, research scientist working in a lab or as an entrepreneur. One could be working in mining and exploration, processing industry like oil, cement, fertilizer or food processing plant. One could also be working in a call centre/back office on day/night duty. However, personnel engaged in Defence/Securities and Policing duties have not been covered in this book, as their role is very specialized and they are often staying far away from their families.

♦ **Place of Living.** It is possible that one is living in a village, a small town or a big town and commuting daily to do his/her job in a distant town, city or a metro city. The distance to the workplace and types of road/rail routes will decide one's time management. If possible, one should select a place for living which suits both the person and his/her spouse. Likewise, sometime schooling of children is important consideration, as one may have to drop and pick up the student.

♦ **Family Type and Size.** Depending upon one's age and society, one could be just living as single or married, having children or having old parents also staying in a joint family. Unlike USA and Europe, most of the Asian and African have relatively bigger families and 30% to 40% live as joint family.

♦ **Job Selection.** Type of job and salary will be as per one's qualification, skill set and experience. Location of job will be as per availability of vacancy. However, one has a major role to play in selection of one's job and place of living to make it a success. Type of job, salary, working hours and computing time are important to the family. If both husband and wife are working, time management at home is different than if wife is a house wife/home-maker and staying at home. Job and family are both important and have to go side by side. Therefore, selection of job by the working members is very important consideration for balancing of work and home life.

♦ **Clear Goal Setting.** One should identify what is important in his/her life. When one is clear what he/she wants, it will be easier to balance work and family life. Set realistic and achievable goals. Follow SMART (Specific, Measurable, Achievable, Realistic and Time Bound) strategy. One must define one's priorities for both job and personal life. Knowing one's qualifications, skill set and work experience, one should decide what one wants to achieve in a near future and in long term (Life Time).

♦ **Prepare To-Do lists.** One must prepare To-Do lists of tasks to be completed in a day, in a week or in a month.

♦ **Prioritize Tasks.** Use techniques like the Eisenhower Matrix or the ABCDE method to prioritize tasks based on urgency and importance.

♦ **Schedule Intelligently.** Develop a daily or weekly schedule that includes work tasks, family commitments and personal time. Stick to this schedule as closely as possible.

♦ **Periodic Review.** One should periodically revisit the schedule and ensure one has enough time to take care of one's work as well as family responsibilities. Using a table calendar will keep one on track so that work time doesn't extend into family time

♦ **Need for Up Skilling.** One should check if his/her present job or higher job or a new job elsewhere, requires learning new skills. If so, one need to find time for learning those missing skills and fill the gaps in one's CV.

♦ **Identify one's best time to work.** One should identify the time of the day when one is most productive and focused. Use that time for important and more complex tasks.

♦ **Time Blocks.** Allocate specific numbers of time blocks say of 30 or 45 or 60 minutes each for different activities.

♦ **Minimize Distraction.** It can be tempting to check personal email, browse social media and respond to pop-ups/notifications, appearing on one's workstation or browsing other unauthorized websites. All these wasteful activities eat up valuable time meant for important tasks. Therefore, it is important to turn off notifications, close unnecessary tabs on the computer/laptop/workstation and create a distraction-free environment to enhance productivity. One should analyze one's daily activities and spend time only on those activities which have positive impact on one's productivity and family wellbeing.

♦ **Learn when to say NO.** Learning when to say NO to additional work is essential for ensuring work-life balance. If one always says "yes" to every task or project, he/she and the team will be soon overloaded and may feel stressed. To avoid this, one should examine existing schedule and make sure one has spare time before accepting additional work. If there is no cushion, explain to the boss/customers and thank them for considering.

♦ **Frank Communication.** An open communication with your boss and the family can help to find a schedule that suits best for the job and the family. If one is having issues at home, one should be frank with the boss and request his/her permission to work from home, on certain days. One needs to discuss possible solutions for meeting both requirements, at the workplace and at home.

- **Hobby as stress Reliever.** One should have time for the hobbies to relieve stress. It could be reading a book/magazine, sketching, photography, bird-watching or solving puzzles .This will improve focus and mitigate anxiety.

- **Healthy Eating habits [9].** Eating healthy, well-balanced meals can help you manage stress by strengthening your immune system, improving your mood and reducing blood pressure.

- **Working Spouse.** The spouse could also be working in some other place with different job timings. In such cases, both husband and wife need to adjust and support each other. One of the two may have to drop small children in a crèche/school and then go to the workplace.

- **Mode of Travel.** One could be using chartered bus of one's organization or public/private bus or a private taxi or rail/metro or a ship/boat or even rope-ways (Available in certain hilly areas). One could be living in a big town, metro-city and having own vehicle to travel to the workplace. One has to plan and reach on time in the workplace and back at home.

- **Commuting Time.** In today's hustle bustle, one need to organize one's mode of travel and type of route so that one reaches safely and on-time at one's workplace. Depending upon the distance, route conditions and type of vehicle, one may take 30 minutes to two hours to reach one's workplace. Irrespective of the mode of travel, one needs to get ready fast and eat breakfast, pick up one's office bag and leave home well in time to reach the pick-up point, metro station/rail station/ bust stop or Jetty in case of ferry (boat service). If one is travelling by company chartered vehicle or by public transport , one need to be on-time at the pickup point and do some reading during travel, However, if one is travelling in own vehicle, one should plan carefully and have a contingency plan to cater for road blocks and weather conditions. One should keep in mind, Expected Time of Arrival (ETA) at one's workplace. Following points need to be considered if commuting by road.

♦ **Distance and Type of Road**. Expressway/ Highway/Normal 4 lanes road will determine safe driving speed.

♦ **Number of Toll Plazas.** Number of times one has to slow down and pay fee at the barriers/toll plazas. Today, prepaid badges are available which can be stuck on wind screen of the vehicle to smoothly go through the toll plaza,

♦ **Number of Red lights.** Each red light intersection point could take 1-3 minutes. One has to account for such delays.

♦ **Speed Limits.** Based on type of vehicle, average driving speed on highways could be 60-90 Km/ hour. One has to drive at safe speed and reach the workplace or home on time.

♦ **Terrain**. It could be Plane, Desert, Jungle, Mountainous or Costal area. The terrain affects driving time and one should take that into consideration.

♦ **Weather.** It could be bright sunshine, cloudy/ drizzling, raining or snowing. This also impacts driving time and one needs to take that into account.

- **Automate Small Tasks**. Automate repetitive tasks both at the workplace and at home to free one's time for more important and creative activities.

- **Set Time Limits**. Clearly define the travel time, work hours and family time. Try to stick to this schedule and avoid work spilling over into family time.

- **Avoid carrying work home.** [8] One should not mix up job and family life. One must finish assigned job day by day at the workplace. This is important because one's work may be linked to the work of other team members and one's delay will cause delays for others as they are waiting for the input to proceed further with their job. If due to any special reason there is pending work for the day, do not carry backlog home. Instead, inform all team members who are affected by such delay and next day reach the workplace early and complete the pending work.

- **Prioritize work**. Identify what are important tasks in the workplace and for the family at home. Plan your time to carry out those tasks as per their priorities.

- **Flexi Working Hours**. One should communicate with the employer to seek permission for having flexi hours. One should discuss flexible work arrangements with the employer, such as working from home, flexible working hours, or reduced hours with reasons.

- **Set Boundaries**. It's essential to establish boundaries. Clearly define work hours and family time. Try to stick to this schedule to avoid work spilling over into family time, It is important to inform your workmates about your availability after working hours. Do not carry office work to home. Try to avoid checking work emails and WhatsApp messages while at home. One should only respond to anything emergent. Likewise, one should inform family members and friends not to ring up at the workplace until there is some emergency.

♦ **Options of flexible hours.** One can explore if flexible working options are available in the organization. If this option is available, one should request to work from home on certain days a week to save on commute time.

♦ **Working from Home**. Post Corona pandemic, many employers have reduced their office/parking spaces and prefer going lean. They encourage their employees working from home. However, it is important that if one is working from home, he/she must ensure that as per scheduled timing, one is on the job and not doing household chores.

♦ **Delegate tasks**. One should not feel to be "know-all" and try to do most jobs oneself. One may be knowledgeable but one cannot handle many jobs concurrently. Hence, inviting more jobs in one's tray, one will become bottle neck in the workflow. This will cause delays for others. One should not be shy to ask for help from own team members, family members, or colleagues. By delegating certain tasks judiciously to other members, one can get some time for doing more important work or do lateral-thinking for idea generation.

♦ **Health care.** Good health is very important for doing any job efficiently, both at the workplace and at home. Therefore, one should take good care of one's physical as well as mental health to ensure one has the required energy to effectively carry out job as well as family responsibilities.

- **Have Good Night Sleep.** When one has a stressful day at work, his/her body needs time to mentally and physically recoup. Getting a sound sleep of 5-6 hours at night can ensure one stays energized and productive for whole day.

- **Stress relieving Exercises.** Regular exercise like Yoga or 30 minutes workout in the gym or brisk walking daily for 6-8 Kms can act as good stress-reliever. Another option for managing stress and anxiety is deep breathing and meditation for 20-30 minutes. These activities get your mind off work and improve your mood and your overall health.

- **Have a good Holiday.** Most organizations give Leave Travel Allowance (LTA) once a year for their employees and their families to go on long holiday. In addition, there are many holidays like weekend, religious/festival days and government holidays. People take a long break when their children and . family members are free to travel on long holiday. When going with family on long holiday, avoid carrying Laptop or office work to the hotel room, as that will spoil the holiday. When planning holiday with family, be far away from home and city hustle bustle. Be totally free and have a great time with the family.

- **Home Leaving Time.** One should leave home for the workplace on right time and every day, giving five minutes cushion to cater for unforeseen delay. It is very important to leave home on a happy note and must not have argument with the spouse, children or elders (if joint family). Always pick up office bag, car keys/office keys and lunch tiffin box and say bye with a smile. Give a hug to kids and elders before closing the door.

♦ **Workplace Arriving Time.** Always plan to reach workplace at least five minutes before the scheduled time. Remember having reached the workplace one must quickly check in and be on the work desk at the scheduled office time.

♦ **Workplace Leaving Time.** Ensure that all work for day has been completed and get ready to leave for home as per office timings. Since one could be pooling transport or leaving by chartered bus, one must be at the designated pick up point on time.

♦ **Home Reaching Time.** While leaving workplace and commuting back home, one should be happy and expect good reception at the door of the house. One should reach home on expected time and greet family members, who have been waiting for the whole day for arrival of their dear one. As one reaches home and press the bell, there may be some family member to open the door. One must say hello and give a hug to all those who were at home waiting for their dear one. One should not rush to the bed room to unload one's bag/briefcase and switch on TV.

♦ **Quality of Time.** It's not always about the amount of time one spends with one's family, but the quality of that time for enjoying together as a family. Make the most of the time with one's loved ones by being fully involved.

♦ **Sharing Home load.** One should not be afraid to ask for help from one's partner, family members, and even children to share some load. Sharing household load can help one some spare time for carrying out other responsibilities of the family.

♦ **Engage a Help.** Domestic help as a maid/servant is easily available in most Asian/African countries. One could engage part- time or full- time servant, as per requirement, and affordability. This way, one can have some spare time to do other important jobs,

Summary. There in no one standard strategy "one-fit-all" to take care of above mentioned types/levels of jobs and family environment. Hence, finding a balance between the job and family is a personal effort and based on personal habits, discipline and motivation. It may require some trial and error to find out what works the best. One should be kind and tolerant with family members and make suitable adjustments as needed to create a happy family life.

Time balancing helps in having successful career and happy family life. One needs to prepare daily and weekly "To Do" lists, prioritize various tasks, and allocate time blocks judiciously. In addition, in each job, there can be different levels, responsibilities and competence requirement. Similarly, type and size of family and society in which one lives could be varying and one need to try out various approaches and find which suits the most.

BIBLIOGRAPHY

1. Alex Gorvachev, Fearless Innovation. John Wiley & Sons, 2020, PP 37-38.

2. Carmine Gallo, The Innovation Secrets of Steve Jobs, McGraw Hill books, 2010, PP 10, 75, 95.

3. Christy Wright, Take Back your Time ", Ramsey Press, 2022, PP 67.

4. Don S Kennedy, Time Management for Entrepreneurs", Entrepreneurs Press, 2013, PP 27, 52

5. Elizabeth Grace Saunders. The 3 Secrets to Effective Time Investment, McGraw Hill, 2013, PP 37.

6. Jason Jennings & Laurence Haughton, It is not the Big that eats the Small; it is the Fast that eats the Slow, Harper Business, 2000, PP 201-203.

7. Jonathan Fields, Uncertainty, Penguin Books, India, 2011, PP 69-71.

8. Malhotra JP, 5 Ways to take care of one hundred fifty situations, Print.com, 2021, PP 6,14, 21,27,32, 46, 61,76,89,142.

9. Martin Manser, Time management Secrets, Collins, London, 2010, 10-22, 26-34, 40, 52, 110-118.

10. Phillip Kotler, Marketing 4.0 – Moving from Traditional to Digital, Wiley, 2017. PP 83.

11. PMI, PMBOK, Guide 5th Edition, PMI Global Inc., 2010, PP 44-46.

12. Ravindra K Tulsyan, How to Eat Elephant?,   S h r o f f publishers & Distributors, New Delhi, 2007, PP 3,14, 40

13. Sarbjit Singh, Career Challenges during Global uncertainties. Notion Press 2018, PP 253-255.

14. Sarbjit Singh, Ride Technology Wave for Career Success, Notion Press, 2021, PP 252-255, 270-272.

15. Sarbjit Singh, Knowledge Sharing Key to Assured Success, Notion Press, 2024, PP 88-90, 202, 209.

16. Stephen Covey, Peter Druker, Warren Bennis, "The Guru Guide", John Wiley & Sons, Inc., 1998, PP 87, 90.

17. Timothy Willink, Time Management, Self-management academy. 2019. PP 3, 18.

Dr. Ssrbjit Singh

Today, we are living amidst fast-developing technologies, digital economies, global uncertainty and fast changing geopolitical scenario. In such turbulent environment, time is the most critical resource to be managed effectively. Time is vital resource but limited to just 24 hours/day. Out of this, we get just 8-10 hours for doing our job at our workplace. Fortunately, with global connectivity through affordable and reliable internet, time-zone difference has become a boon, where we can work round the clock and across the globe.

The book provides jargon-free, compact and easy-to-grasp material for young Professionals, Team-Leaders and Managers, Educationists, Doctors/Support staff, Researchers to use their time more effectively. This book will also help CEO/CTO and senior management to invest more in training their young professionals to use of their time more effectively.

The book suggests the reader to fully know own job, do self-analysis of own and team competency, how one is utilizing his/her available time and how to delegate/outsource certain tasks. It also suggests when and how to say "Firm No" to the time-distractors. This book will help the reader to become more time conscious, more productive and popular among team members, seniors, customers and business partners. The reader will soon start balancing time for the work and family.